ANGUS

FIONA C. SCHARLAU

The History Press

First published 2009

The History Press
The Mill, Brimscombe Port
Stroud, Gloucestershire, GL5 2QG
www.thehistorypress.co.uk

British Library Cataloguing in Publication Data.
A catalogue record for this book is available from the British Library.

ISBN 978 0 7509 5089 3

Typesetting and origination by The History Press
Printed in India by Nutech Print Services

CONTENTS

ACKNOWLEDGEMENTS

The author would like to offer her sincere thanks to all who assisted in making this book happen. The team at Angus Archives were patient with all my mutterings and enthusiastic cries of 'look at this one!'. Karen at Arbroath Library was even more patient and extremely helpful in locating elusive facts from the newspapers. Brechin Library and Montrose Museum staff also have my thanks for their help – and for the biscuits. Kate at the Gallery Team is owed a huge thank you for her scans. Margaret, Donna, Elizabeth, Helen, Norman and Bruce all gave their time to read through the manuscript, and point out the typing errors, errant commas and other silliness on my part. And lastly, my thanks go to the readers at Angus Archives who did not always know that the information they conveyed would be of such great help. There will be chocolates for you all.

Feeding the swans at Friockheim Dam on the Lunan Water.

INTRODUCTION

The county of Angus is situated between Dundee in the south and Aberdeenshire in the north. It was part of the ancient kingdom of the Picts which was taken over by the Scots in the late ninth century. Angus probably originated from the Scots house of that name, although it was also the name of two Pictish kings.

The name Angus was used until approximately 1650, when the Cromwellian government introduced the term Forfarshire, after the county town of Forfar. However, Angus (-shire) continued to be a popular name amongst mapmakers who frequently favoured it over the official name. By 1928 the county council bowed to popular pressure and officially re-instated the ancient name of Angus. Until the local government reorganisation of 1975, the city of Dundee was part of the county of Angus.

Angus has been described as Scotland in miniature: it has seaside settlements, glens and mountains, busy ports and thriving inland towns and villages, all surrounded by some of the best agricultural land in Scotland.

The strong individual identities of the Angus towns and villages have been recognised for a long time. The *Montrose Directory* of 1885 reprinted a humourous article written in 1825, in which it gently pokes fun at the different characteristics of Arbroath, Brechin and Montrose. One claim was that, 'The genius of the Montrose folks lies in dress, show and, above all, respectability. That of Arbroath in turning the penny to advantage. In Brechin, every weaver is a philosopher.'

The character of each town and village has much to do with its origins. Forfar was a favourite royal residence of the sons of King Malcolm III and his queen (later Saint) Margaret, even before it was granted a charter as a royal burgh. Montrose is a royal burgh with an international port, and its role as a trading centre allowed its merchants to flourish on trade with the Baltic, Holland, France and the Caribbean. Arbroath was synonymous with the medieval abbey founded by King William I in 1178. Brechin's origin also lies in a religious foundation which was granted by King Malcolm II between 971-95, and Brechin Cathedral – which dates back to the early twelfth century, when its Round Tower was built – is regarded as the mother church of Angus. Kirriemuir is an ancient burgh of barony, held by the Earls of Angus and now famous as the birthplace of both author J.M. Barrie and rock musician Bon Scott of AC/DC. In 1797 Carnoustie was carved out of the sandy Links when Thomas Lowson took the first feu of the village after a dream. Monifieth had to fight for its unique identity in 1905 when an amalgamation with the nearby city of Dundee was proposed. The fishing village of Auchmithie clings to the cliff top while Ferryden hangs its laundry out on poles over the river. Edzell is widely regarded as one of the prettiest villages in Scotland with its great attention to gardens and hanging baskets. Letham is a popular village, planned and created from an unproductive Muir.

Many notable characters were born and brought up in Angus. The most famous natives are probably Queen Elizabeth, the Queen Mother from Glamis and the author of *Peter Pan*,

J.M. Barrie from Kirriemuir. There are many others who gained acknowledgment for their achievements, such as; Revd Patrick Bell of Carmyllie who invented the reaping machine, Robert Watson-Watt who discovered the science underlying radar during the Second World War, Sir Hector Munro of Lindertis who measured mountains, and Charles Lyell of Kinnordy, geologist and friend of Charles Darwin.

Some, however, did not gain credit for their inventions. James Chalmers of Arbroath proposed the adhesive postage stamp three years before the introduction of the penny post in 1840, but failed to win recognition for his idea. The same fate befell James Bowman Lindsay, another Carmyllie man, one of many inventors to produce an effective incandescent light bulb long before Eddison produced them commercially.

Angus has also produced a great number of writers, from J.M. Barrie to Scots-language poets Hugh MacDiarmid and Violet Jacob, and artists William Lamb, David Waterson, Colvin Smith and George Paul Chalmers to name a few.

The life, work and people of Angus are visible in the Angus Photographic Archive, part of the wider collections held at Angus Archives, located in a building adjacent to the ancient Priory of Restenneth. This is an appropriate location for an archive because the priory, according to Scottish historian Hector Boece, housed the royal records of Scotland for a time.

The images selected for *Angus In Old Photographs* were chosen by the author and are an individual, and sometimes quirky, choice representing, in her humble opinion, some of the best images held by the Angus Photographic Archive; all but a few images have never been published before.

The Angus Photographic Archive is a work in progress, and dependent on donations for its expansion and ability to record all facets of Angus, modern and old. Some aspects of Angus and Angus life are simply not yet represented. Other areas, especially the larger towns such as Arbroath and Brechin, have been well covered. The work of local photographers, such as Brechin photographer John M. Dunn, who delighted in capturing candid shots of travellers and town councillors, is frequently used. Internationally-acclaimed William Anckorn of Arbroath, who took fabulous images of the Auchmithie fishing community, is not as well represented as we might like owing to the small number of his images in the public domain. Highly talented amateurs such as John Fraser of Arbroath took many well-observed photographs of the fisher community at work. Many, many images are taken by enthusiastic and unknown amateurs. All of them help us to see what life was like in Angus, how much it has changed and how much it has remained the same.

The Angus Photographic Archive records the images of Angus people, their houses, their work places, where they played and how they entertained themselves and visitors to the area. There is no such thing as too many photographs, so if you have an image you would like to donate or share, please contact Angus Archives at angus.archives@angus.gov.uk

Fiona C. Scharlau, Angus Archives, 2009

1

PLACES

Milton of Monifieth was once the centre of a busy village and industrial centre. The origins of the Monifieth foundry of James F. Low & Co. Ltd were here, beginning with the marriage of Jane Fairweather to William Low, a spinning wheel manufacturer at the Milton. William had ambitions to start a foundry and needed plans for machinery. His brother-in-law George was an artist. William therefore sent George to work in various English mills where he could spy on and draw the machinery. George drew the machine parts onto little 10in pieces of paper which he concealed in his hat. William and Jane reputedly gave him a new hat every year in honour of his contribution to the new company. The Low Foundry went on to expand over the next century before finally closing in the 1980s.

The village of Monifieth has changed little over the centuries. For many years it was mainly inhabited by farmers who rented small plots ('pendicles') from the Panmure Estate and made their living by selling dairy produce in the neighbouring city of Dundee. Monifieth, with its fresh sea air, had a very agreeable climate with few epidemics and many of its inhabitants lived to a very advanced age. Its seaside location made it popular as a holiday resort and day trip destination from Dundee, which was just a short train ride away. In 1895 the village adopted the Police Act and became a burgh.

In 1914 the city of Dundee tried to annex the neighbouring villages of Monifieth and Broughty Ferry. A hearing was held at the House of Commons in April 1914 and Monifieth Town Council argued that the burgh had a separate economic existence from Dundee. They cited the two foundries, which between them employed almost 1,000 people. The Town Council won the case at a cost of £24,000.

Barry Buddon on the Tay estuary has been a military training camp for over 100 years.
It was originally leased from the Panmure Estate by the Forfarshire Rifle Volunteers in the
mid-nineteenth century, and in 1897 the Earl of Panmure sold the land, totalling 2,300
acres, to the War Office. Approximately 30,000 military personnel pass through its ranges
every year. This view shows artillery training during the First World War.

A view along
Carnoustie's High
Street showing
the Young
Men's Christian
Association
building on the
left in the 1920s.
The YMCA
relocated to
the High Street
from nearby
Bonella Street in
1875. In 1881
a bazaar was
held in Dundee
to raise funds for
the construction
work, but there
were insufficient
funds to complete the exterior and a temporary wood and plaster front had to be erected. By
the time of this photograph the new frontage had been completed. It was a popular venue for
indoor entertainments of all kinds, housing the Pierrot shows in 1922 when the season was
a washout. Amongst other things, the building has been used as a debating club, a billiards
room, and a roller rink in the 1930s.

Graham Place, Carnoustie.

In Edwardian times the west end of Carnoustie consisted of a few scattered homes, such as these in Graham Place, now part of Wallace Street. These fields where oat stooks are drying are now covered by post-Second World War housing developments. Carnoustie Town Council purchased farms such as Wards Farm in order to build housing to answer demand for homes from Dundee overspill and general growth.

Westhaven, a former fishing village, has now blended into the expanding boundaries of Carnoustie and yet retains its distinctive atmosphere. The fishermen of the village utilized natural rock pools as a harbour for small fishing boats. Enterprising fishermen often had a good sideline in taking tourists out for boat trips.

Danger Point, at the Fit o' the Toon in Arbroath, is aptly named because of the danger to the buildings there from high seas and storms. However, the sea was not the only danger to this area. In 1781 the town was subjected to a pirate attack by Captain Fall and his ship the *Fearnought*, which bombarded the Fit o' the Toon with canon fire while holding the town to ransom. The militia was called, and after a day Fall called off the attack and sailed away empty handed.

Arbroath's harbour was built by order of the Abbot of Arbroath in the medieval period. It was small and not greatly suited to trade. A replacement, commissioned and built around 1725, greatly improved trade, allowing Arbroath ships to trade with the American colonies, Holland, the Baltic and France. Improvements to the harbour continued over the years including the addition of a lighthouse at the entrance, and a patent slip, which provided a cheaper alternative to a dry dock for ship repairs. The last major building work was the outer harbour in 1839. This allowed Arbroath's weaving and shipbuilding industries to take off as their products were shipped worldwide. Today, the harbour still houses some fishing boats and operates as a marina.

Arbroath's fishing fleet remain behind the shelter of the sturdy harbour wall during a storm. The fleet included many herring fishing boats. Since 1826 Arbroath's magistrates had actively encouraged fishermen from all over Scotland to make their homes in Arbroath by offering them land to build their homes. They chose to settle at the Fit o' the Toon near the harbour, giving this area a distinctive identity. This area also has a distinctive aroma, being the area where the Arbroath Smokie is prepared!

Arbroath has long been a popular seaside town, with sweeping sandy beaches and plenty of entertainment for visitors. The old Cannon Common, now more commonly called the West Common, was the centre of activities. This view was taken in the 1920s prior to the building of the open-air swimming pool and shows the putting green and tennis courts in their former location, along with the wooden hut serving both facilities. Seaforth House and Murray Place are in the background; both are now gone.

Arbroath's High Street connects the abbey precincts to the harbour and the Fit o' the Toon. The High Street accommodated both tenements and the factory of Keith Blackman, although this has now been replaced by a modern set of shops.

The old fishing village of Auchmithie was established in the Middle Ages and was owned by the Earl of Northesk until 1919. In the past, the Earl viewed the Auchmithie fishermen as his personal property and in 1705 successfully stopped some of them moving Arbroath by having them declared serfs by the Privy Council and returned to the village. They had to wait until the early part of the nineteenth century before they could freely move to Arbroath. In its heyday Auchmithie housed about 400 inhabitants and had twenty small boats for catching crabs and lobster, along with twelve large boats for white fishing and six following the herring. This late nineteenth-century photograph by William Anckorn shows a typical village house with a great deal of activity taking place outside, from shelling mussels to baiting the lines.

Auchmithie is set on top of a cliff with a steep path leading down to the harbour. In 1814 Sir Walter Scott visited the village on his east coast tour and stayed at the local inn. Scott immortalized the village in his novel *The Antiquary* as the fictional village of Musselcraig, putting Auchmithie on the literary map ever since. Scott was not the first famous visitor; poet Robert Burns enjoyed breakfast at the inn in 1787 when he travelled the east coast in the course of his duties as an Excise Officer.

The tiny fishing village of Ethie Haven lies almost hidden at the foot of a steep winding road on the southern edge of Lunan Bay. The Ethie Haven fishermen were once engaged in both line fishing and in netting salmon. The salmon rights were owned by Joseph Johnston & Sons Ltd. When steam-powered fishing boats were introduced from the 1880s onwards, villages with no proper landing facilities, such as Ethie Haven, gradually withered as viable fishing villages. Ethie Haven now consists largely of holiday homes, and was one of the very last places in Angus to be connected to mains electricity.

A beautiful view of Ferryden from Rossie Island showing the old Inch Burn. This view no longer exists as the Inch Burn and its channel now lie beneath the South Quay of Montrose harbour. The sluggish burn was filled in during the 1970s to reclaim the land for the construction of an oil support base and further harbour accommodation, and Rossie Island became an island in name only. The island had been the site of an ancient Pictish chapel and graveyard, both of which are now surrounded by modern developments.

The former fishing village of Ferryden and its harbour are no longer recognisable from this view as it has been built up and incorporated into the modern South Quay of Montrose harbour. The village owed its existence to an ancient river crossing and its importance as a fishing village grew throughout the eighteenth and much of the nineteenth centuries, mirroring the growth in herring fishing. Line fishing for white fish, such as haddock and ling, was also important. Ferryden benefited from the establishment of Joseph Johnston & Sons Ltd as salmon fishers and fish curers with broad trading interests.

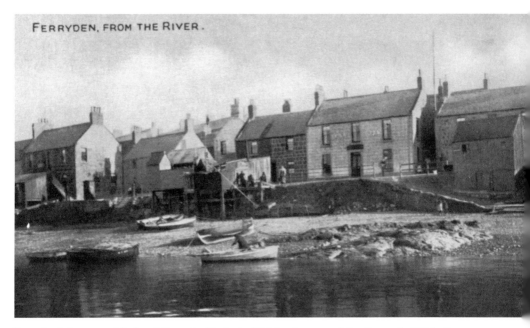

FERRYDEN, FROM THE RIVER.

Ferryden's fortunes ebbed and flowed with that of fishing in general. By the early 1920s the Ferryden fleet was in serious decline. Like many other small fishing ports, it had been unable to re-establish its market after the First World War. Commercial fishing had all but ceased by 1930, with the exception of a handful of boats.

A view of Montrose from the west of Ferryden over the River South Esk, now no longer visible. The square ruin of the ancient Rossie Island chapel can be seen adjacent to the ship-building yard, at the very edge of the island. A number of tall ship's masts are visible, as are a number of tall industrial chimneys.

This is a delightful view over to Montrose, the road bridge and the tidal basin, with the hills beyond. It was taken from Ferryden beach, on the site of the present day South Quay. The concrete bridge was built in the 1930s and replaced by a new bridge in 2005.

There have now been four bridges crossing from Rossie Island over the South Esk to the town of Montrose. Prior to the first bridge, traffic had to cross the river by boat, or make the long journey around the basin. The first bridge opened to traffic in 1795. During the 1790s, local landowner Hercules Ross of Rossie, who owned the rights to the ferry, fought a long battle with Montrose Town Council for compensation for the loss of his ferry trade. As a mark of protest, the ferrymen walked across the new bridge, carrying their oars draped in black, as a symbol of the death of the ferry.

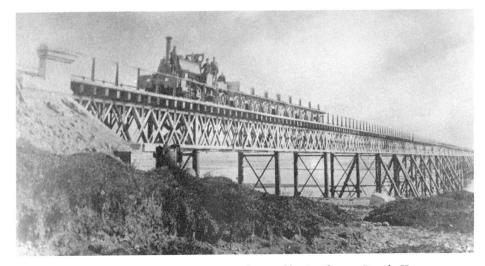

The first railway bridge over the South Esk was designed by Sir Thomas Bouch. He was responsible for the design of the railway bridge over the River Tay, which fell down on 28 December 1879, leading to the deaths of seventy-five people. After this event, the Montrose railway bridges were tested and the bridge over the main channel was found to be faulty. The two bridges were demolished and replaced by the bridges in service today. This train and its driver and engineers have stopped on the bridge to pose for the photographer. This bridge was demolished before it carried any commercial traffic.

Montrose boasts the widest High Street in Scotland. This panoramic view, looking towards the basin, was taken by local photographer William Rodger from the steeple of the parish church in around 1860. The vantage point shows a fine display of the old gable-ended buildings which gave Montrosians their nickname of gable-enders. A few of these gable ends have survived but many have disappeared to make way for large Victorian buildings, such as the former Central Hotel and the Clydesdale Buildings, and to open up Hume Street in order to provide easier access to the railway station, yet the character of the High Street remains largely unchanged.

This view illustrates the nature of Montrose High Street, retaining much of its original medieval shape. As wide as it is today, it was once wider; the town council permitted a number of planned encroachments on the street over the centuries. A row of old market booths once ran down the centre of the street, becoming more permanent but rather ramshackle. In the eighteenth century the magistrates became obsessed with the beautification of the town and this mid row was demolished. Their position is marked by the line of plant beds dividing the street today.

A view of Montrose High Street looking south to the Town House and to the parish church beyond. The Town House was constructed in 1763 to allow the burgh magistrates more room to hold their meetings and also to provide the local gentry and merchants with rooms in which they could hold assemblies. Soon after it was constructed it was deemed to be inadequate and more money was raised to add another floor and a bigger Assembly Room. Poor construction meant that the floor of this Assembly Room was not properly supported from below and in the 1960s the room ceased to be used for public occasions. It is now, after renovation, used as offices.

The Mid Links of Montrose is a wide area of landscaped park created from a 'wild open space' of communal grazing which was said to be a quagmire in winter and a dust bowl in summer. Its transformation into something more elegant and beautiful was largely due to the vision and determination of Provost George Scott, a professional gardener. He decided it was his mission to civilise this wild area, and in 1875 began working on the individual parks from south towards the north.

Usan, or Ullishaven as it was once known, was a small fishing community to the south of Ferryden. The village was established by the thirteenth century to provide salmon for the king when he was in residence in his castle in Forfar. The cadger, or fish seller, was a privileged royal servant and no man could tamper with his duties without incurring the severest punishment. One local baron attempted to interfere with the delivery of the royal salmon and was tried and executed for his crime. Later the village took on coastguard duties. The watchtower was rented to the coastguard from 1835 and used up to around the 1920s. The village steadily declined and the houses became roofless and derelict.

A view of Forfar Loch looking over the Myre, as seen from the steeple of Forfar parish church in the late 1800s. Forfar Loch is free of later housing developments. The Myre is the grassy area between the houses on the left and Craik's Manor Works factory on the right. Before drainage of the loch started in the 1760s the water came right up to the back walls of many High Street and Castle Street properties. Many houses still have fishing rights to the Myre, most of which is now a car park, written into their title deeds.

Another fascinating view of Victorian Forfar taken from the steeple of the parish church, looking north west past the Myre, or pasture, towards Forfar Loch. The Town House was central to the administration of the town, sitting on the junction of the High Street and Castle Street, with the Town and County Hall behind it. This grand Georgian building replaced the earlier medieval tollbooth, notorious for housing a large number of witch suspects in the 1660s. When the Town House was first built in 1788, a sky walk connected it to the neighbouring inn, now the County Hotel. This idea has been revived in the use of such a passageway to connect the Town House to the Canmore Room in the Town and County Hall.

Forfar divides its High Street into the East High Street and the West High Street. Here we see the site of the old market cross in front of the Town House, looking up the East High Street. Many of these buildings were rebuilt in the Victorian period. However, there are a few earlier survivors. The large building on the left is eighteenth century, with the tell-tale chimney in the middle of the building, and occupies a prominent position on the corner of the High Street and Castle Street. Further up the street is a small white building sitting with its gable end to the pavement. This building is even older, possibly seventeenth century, and represents the old style of building: long, narrow houses with their sides fronting the edge of the medieval burgage plot.

This is an unusual view of the back of the West High Street in Forfar taken from the Myre before the car park was constructed. The back rigs, or long thin strips of garden ground, are clearly seen. Many of the back rigs have now been developed. The Guide Hall stands in the garden ground at the foot of the church. To the left of St Margaret's Church is the old building on the site now occupied by the post office.

In 1885 Kirriemuir's High Street was a quieter place than today and the man with the stall is in no danger of being run over by any traffic. The old Town House, built in 1604, is probably the oldest building in Kirriemuir. It once had outside stairs leading to the upper floors, but these have long been removed. The building retained its original rectangular shape, as shown in this photograph, until the nineteenth century when it was rounded off into its present shape. The building functioned as the court room and jail for the Earls of Angus, who held the burgh as a burgh of barony. Today it provides a museum for the town and its environs.

Cobbles fell out of favour as a road surface in the middle of the twentieth century, and the cobbles, or cassies as they were nicknamed, were either lifted or simply covered over with tarmac. A gang of roadmen are at work lifting the cassies from the centre of Kirriemuir. The work was undertaken by William Briggs & Sons Ltd of Dundee.

This view of the Pierhead area of Kirriemuir seems to have been taken from the near the Gairie Burn looking up towards the old houses built around the Kirk Wynd. The old medieval system of long rigs or strips of land behind the houses can still be seen clearly. The centre of the photograph is dominated by an old cottage set amongst a number of kitchen gardens. Kirriemuir-born author J.M. Barrie created the town's alter ego of Thrums in his Scottish stories for a London newspaper (hence the label on the photograph).

A view of the commonty in Kirriemuir, an area of common land once used as a bleaching green. The town is fortunate in having a number of green spaces, such as the Kirriemuir Public Park, which was formed when the Den of Glasswell was purchased and laid out as a park. The trustees aimed to extend the park by acquiring the other side of the Den from the Kinnordy estate. The intention was to form a skating pond within easy distance of the town. To raise the money necessary the trustees held a Grand Fancy Bazaar in September 1880. Here we see two little girls strolling down the path while another lady sketches. The chimney stack of J.D. Wilkie's weaving factory can be seen in the background.

Brechin's High Street could not have been more crowded than on the day the town celebrated the jubilee of Queen Victoria in 1887. In the centre of the scrum, members of a Masonic lodge can just be made out. Others are more comfortably accommodated at an upper window. Some people are flying flags from the upper windows of John Clark's shop. Adjacent to this shop is one of Brechin's surviving seventeenth-century gable-ended buildings.

The junction of High Street and Church Street is an important site within Brechin. The old market cross stood here until 1767, on the spot marked by the cast-iron lamp post. The High Street is very steep and was originally terraced to make it easier to navigate. In 1789 the medieval tollbooth was replaced by a new Town House with funds raised by public subscription and donations from the merchant Guildry. The building included not

only a Guild Hall for meetings and assemblies, but also a courtroom and a jail. All too soon the Town House proved inadequate for the administrative needs of the burgh, and in 1894 the new Municipal Buildings were opened in Bank Street.

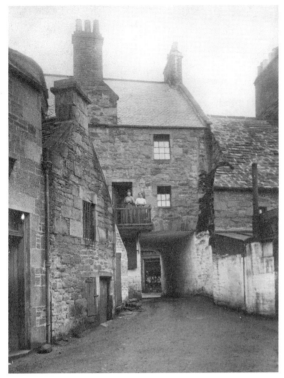

The pend, or covered passageway, leading from the High Street to Bishop's Close, Brechin, has always been a favourite spot for photographers. The pend led into the medieval cathedral's precincts. The bishop had his palace at this end of the site. A church has stood here since Pictish times when the Round Tower was built, around the tenth century. A church community grew up around this church and eventually a town grew up around the Chanonry to service the needs of the cathedral canons. Even to this day the Chanonry area retains a unique identity.

The Den and its nursery looking over to St Columba Church and Southesk Street, Brechin. The grounds in the Den adjacent to the nursery were acquired by the Parochial Board in 1856 for a new burial ground. George Henderson of the Den Nurseries was as much a landscape designer as a seedsman. He designed much of the open space and parks in Brechin. The Parochial Board was responsible for building the bridge over the Den for access to the new cemetery. Ground was also developed for the Brechin Infirmary.

St Ninian's Square, Brechin is now an elegant tree-lined square, but it was once on the edge of the town and enjoyed a more rural ambience. Here we see long-horned cattle in front of a water trough and a small fountain. The Shambles, or slaughterhouse, was once located on the edge of this area before its removal further afield. The square was the subject of improvements in the 1890s when electric lights were installed, seating added, and the Gardner Memorial Church and library were built.

A rare view of the Inch at Brechin taken from the south side of the dam over the River South Esk, with the houses on River Street beyond. The Inch has long been an industrial site and has housed a bleaching and wash house, a paper mill and the Meikle Mill. The Inch Bleach Field was the business venture of David Scott of Newington House and John Lamb in the 1860s. They employed about 100 people on wages varying from 14s for a man to 7s for a woman. The paper mill employed seventy people producing up to 500 tons of cartridge paper and newspaper.

123 Panmure Hotel and High Street, Edzell.

The Panmure Arms Hotel in the village of Edzell sits at the crossroads leading to Glen Lethnot and Glenesk. The view is largely the same today. The Panmure Arms Hotel was originally built when the village began flourishing as a tourist resort after the railway was constructed. The village promoted itself as 'the healthiest place in Scotland.' It was a popular place for day trippers to the glens to stop for refreshment.

The Dalhousie Arch in Edzell tells a sad story; it commemorates not only the death of the local landowner, the Earl of Dalhousie, but also that of his wife. They died within a few hours of each other in November 1887. The arch was erected by tenants of the Dalhousie estate in 1889 to commemorate this event. The couple were held in very high esteem because of their devotion and personal attention to the affairs of their tenants. The arch spans 10ft and provides a magnificent entrance to the village with its wide High Street. Before too much motor traffic passed under the arch, it was an ideal place for playing cricket.

A quiet scene on Edzell's High Street where two ladies are enjoying a stroll, while chatting and knitting. Much of Edzell was planned as a garden village and so benefited from wide streets and generous gardens. It was a popular holiday resort in the last years of the nineteenth century. A legacy of this era is found in the village gardens, where many large garden sheds have survived. These were built as accommodation for families who rented out their homes during the summer.

Letham is one of a small number of planned villages in Angus. It was created by George Dempster, the owner of the Dunnichen estate and a Member of Parliament. When he inherited the estate it was still farmed in the medieval style of run-rigs (long thin strips of land) with in-fields and out-fields. Dempster set out to take advantage of new ideas in agriculture and in planning. On 5 July 1788 the former farm of Letham, set on an unproductive muir, was set out as a new town which flourished as a centre of the linen industry. As the weaving trade declined, the village was well placed to thrive as part of the wider agricultural community.

The pretty little village of Kingoldrum lies four miles west of Kirriemuir on the road to Glenisla. *The New Statistical Account* of 1845 described the people of the parish as 'obliging, hospitable and affable,' while praising them for being checked in their salmon poaching habits of old. The main business of the parish was agriculture, specialising in black-faced sheep and in Angus-shire black cattle.

The village of Glamis is often overlooked by the fame of its nearby castle, the former home of Queen Elizabeth, the Queen Mother. The castle is a relative newcomer compared to the antiquity of the village. The manse garden contains a beautiful carved Pictish stone, which is more than a 1,000 years old. It was carved with a large Celtic cross on one side and Pictish symbols such as a large salmon, a mirror and two fighting men on the other. In AD 844 the Scots King Kenneth took over the Picts kingdom and with it came the gradual introduction of Christianity. Glamis is linked with the Irish bishop St Fergus, who settled in Glamis to convert the 'barbarous' Picts to Christianity.

The little ruined church on the edge of Loch Lee at the very end of Glenesk is ancient. It was founded in AD 800 by St Drostan, and was in use until the new parish church was constructed in 1803. Loch Lee's beauty has inspired many day trippers to make the mile-long walk down the cart track to reach the ruins from the equally ruined Invermark Castle.

Angus has over fifty parishes, each with their own churches. The origins of many of these parishes lie in the early Middle Ages. As the centuries passed medieval chapels were no longer suitable or big enough and were rebuilt. The eighteenth century was a period of 'beautification' and improvements. Newtyle's church was just such an example. A chapel existed on the site since 1242 and was replaced by a Georgian church in 1767, as shown here, with Kirkton farm's stackyard in the background. It subsequently burned down in 1867, and was replaced with the present Victorian building. Many of the old gravestones in the cemetery were removed and recycled as paving stones and gateposts during the 1960s.

Old Cross and Square, Fowlis

Due to numerous boundary changes some areas that are now in Angus were once part of Perthshire. Fowlis Easter is one such village. The village is most famous for the rare Pre-Reformation wall paintings in its parish church.

Arbirlot village once flourished as a centre of the handloom weaving trade, supporting upwards of thirty handlooms in the early years of the nineteenth century. The webs they weaved were taken every Saturday to Arbroath by a local carrier. This trade was gradually replaced by the new power loom factories established in Arbroath by a new breed of entrepreneur such as Arbirlot weaver Francis Webster, who had left the village and established his own works on the Brothock Burn in Arbroath. The factory thrived for over 100 years weaving sailcloth for the shipping trade.

2

HISTORIC BUILDINGS

Angus has many castles, some of them ruined while others are still home to the families who have lived there for centuries. The most famous of them is Glamis Castle, childhood home of Queen Elizabeth, the Queen Mother. The Bowes Lyon family has lived at Glamis since the fourteenth century. The castle was built on the site of a much earlier royal hunting lodge where King Malcolm II died in 1034 after being wounded in battle nearby. Glamis is well known for the legends relating to a mysterious room in which a monster reputedly once lived. It was bricked up after his death and ever since people have been engaged in counting the windows, trying to locate this hidden room. A Grey Lady also haunts the castle and is believed to be the ghost of Janet, Lady Glamis who was burned alive on a trumped up charge of witchcraft.

CORTACHY CASTLE

Cortachy Castle is the home of the ancient line of Ogilvie Earls of Airlie. Its original function was to guard the entrance to Glen Clova. The earliest parts of the building date back to the fourteenth century although much has been added over many years. Victorian architect David Bryce remodelled much of the building in 1871, presenting it in the baronial style we see today. Cortachy Castle has its share of ghosts too and is said to be haunted by a drummer ghost, who is heard whenever a member of the family dies.

AULDBAR CASTLE, FORFARSHIRE

Auldbar Castle near Brechin was demolished in 1965. The castle was originally a four-storey sixteenth-century tower house, the remains of which are visible to the rear of the photograph. It was enlarged around 1810 in the baronial style. The estate had been owned by the Chalmers family since 1753 when it was purchased by William Chalmers, an Army quartermaster in Gibraltar who also had business interests in the weaving of a coarse linen called after the town of Osnaburg, where it originated.

Another lost building is Anniston House near Inverkeilor, a large country house set in an estate of 978 acres. It was built around 1785 for the Rait family, and was most likely designed by James Playfair, who designed other properties in Angus such as Farnell Church and Forfar Town House. Only the gatehouse and a walled garden remain today.

Farnell Castle is a colourful part of the Angus countryside, rendered in an historic shade of pink lime wash. The castle was the summer residence of the powerful Bishops of Brechin until the Reformation in 1566. After that date it fell into the hands of the Carnegies of Southesk, who live a few miles away at Kinnaird Castle. At one point in its past it was used as an almshouse for old women. The present building, grandly renamed a castle, was built around the early part of the sixteenth century and was left to become derelict on at least two occasions. During the 1960s the building had to be completely gutted to eradicate dry rot and woodworm. Today it is restored and once again used as a private home.

Queen Mary's visit to Edzell in 1921 was not the first by a monarch of that name: Mary, Queen of Scots had stayed in the castle during a Royal progress of 1562. Edzell Castle is an impressive ruin today. The original village of Edzell once lay outside the castle walls, but in the sixteenth century a member of the Lindsay family decided that the village spoiled the view. This led to the relocation of Edzell to the neighbouring village of Slateford, which became known as Edzell. The castle is most famous for its walled garden created by Sir David Lindsay, a well-travelled Renaissance man. The castle also houses wall carvings which date from 1604-1610 and are unique in Scotland. The wall panels represent the planetary deities, the cardinal virtues and the liberal arts. Sir David did not have long to enjoy his splendid garden, dying in 1610 when the work seems to have been hastily finished off.

Lunan Bay is a beautiful sweeping bay of golden sands, crowned by the silhouette of the ruins of Red Castle. The earliest part of the castle was built by King William I of Scotland, a king who favoured Angus for hunting expeditions. The castle fell into decline after 1579 when Lady Elizabeth Beaton took Andrew Gray, a younger man, as her second husband. He fell in love with her daughter, leading to a violent family argument. Elizabeth and her daughter retreated into Red Castle for safety, where they were besieged by Gray for two years. The siege was ended when he burned the inhabitants out of the castle, spelling the end of its use.

Arbroath Abbey was founded by King William I in 1178, and was dedicated to his friend Thomas Beckett, the murdered Archbishop of Canterbury. The seal of the abbey depicts the murder of Becket at the High Altar. The abbey was an important institution in the area. King William had been generous in the financial endowments given to the monks and they held land in every burgh in Scotland and in twenty-four Angus parishes. In addition, they were allowed to institute a market in the town and to build a harbour, setting Arbroath on the path to wealth and prosperity in the future. One of the most important events in Scottish history was the 6 April 1320 Declaration of Arbroath, which asserted Scotland's ancient independence and influenced many future independence declarations around the world.

Brechin Cathedral is an ancient church with a rare Round Tower dating back more than 1,000 years to Pictish times. Most views of the cathedral are commonly taken from Bishop's Close or Church Wynd. This angle is unusual and appears to be taken from the old Manse gardens. After the Reformation the cathedral assumed a new role as the Protestant parish church of Brechin. The first reformed minister, John Hepburn, was an unusual man; he had been the last treasurer of the Catholic cathedral and the eldest illegitimate son of a former Bishop of Brechin.

Restenneth Priory is an ancient ruin once encircled by a loch, now drained. There has been a religious house on the site since at least the eighth century, when King Nechtan called for stonemasons from Northumberland to build him a church in the Roman style. The church was nearly 500 years old when Robert the Bruce buried his infant son Prince John in front of the High Altar. After the Reformation the building slid into a quiet decline. By the nineteenth century much of its stone work had been robbed for stone dykes. The priory suffered the indignity of becoming a cattle pen in the 1800s when a farmer enclosed the old cloister. The picturesque ruin has long been an attraction for visitors. The priory subsequently came into the care of the Works Department, now Historic Scotland.

The Bell Rock, eleven miles off the coast of Arbroath and submerged twice a day under 16ft of water, had always been a grave danger to ships. The medieval abbots of Arbroath ordered the installation of a warning bell, but it was not sufficient for the purpose. Many ships and lives were lost, including all hands of the sixty-four-gun man-of-war HMS *York*. This accident was the catalyst for the construction of a lighthouse on the Bell Rock. Robert Stevenson, the father of *Kidnapped* author Robert Louis Stevenson, was commissioned to undertake the complex construction process. Building work lasted from 1807 to 1811. The lighthouse is still in service today.

No. 9 Brechin Road, Kirriemuir is the birthplace of J.M. Barrie, the creator of *Peter Pan*. Barrie was born on 9 May 1860, one of eight children brought up in this house. It was in the communal wash-house adjacent to the property that Barrie staged his first play, written when he was just seven years old. He charged an entry fee of a marble, a pin or a spinning top. Barrie later revealed that the humble wash-house was the inspiration for the little house built by the Lost Boys for Wendy in Never-Never Land.

Wind power was once an important power source, especially in areas where the water supply was inconsistent in summer. The windmill at Bolshan, or Beauchamp as it was once known, in Kinnell parish was most likely used to power a threshing mill, with wind power replacing horses. It is now one of a handful of windmills surviving in Angus. The farmhouse and buildings occupy much of the site of an ancient castle, chapel and burial ground, the remains of which were all ploughed under sometime before 1767.

Panmure Monument Carnoustie

Left: The Panmure Testimonial Tower can be seen from much of southern Angus. It was built on the Panmure Estate by the grateful tenant farmers of William Ramsay Maule, first Lord Panmure (1771–1852), for his kindness to them in forgoing rents during years of poor harvests in the 1820s (in many cases he cancelled the arrears altogether). The tower was designed by Edinburgh architect John Henderson and completed in 1839.

Below: Much of Angus came out with the Old and Young Pretenders during the Jacobite uprisings of 1715 and 1745 and many lairds rode off to war. The Earl of Panmure rode out in 1715 and he gave instructions that the gates should be barred behind him and never opened again until a Stewart sat on the throne. The uprising failed and many of the landed Jabobite families found their estates were forfeited to the Crown. The Earl of Panmure had to escape to Europe for safety while the countess worked tirelessly to raise money to buy back the estate.

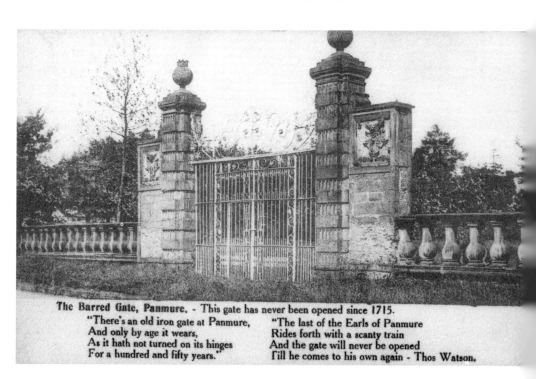

The Barred Gate, Panmure. - This gate has never been opened since 1715.

"There's an old iron gate at Panmure,
And only by age it wears,
As it hath not turned on its hinges
For a hundred and fifty years."

"The last of the Earls of Panmure
Rides forth with a scanty train
And the gate will never be opened
Till he comes to his own again - Thos Watson.

In the 1860s, Forfar constructed a new Sheriff Court and prison on the edge of the Market Muir. The Sheriff Court is an imposing Gothic building, while the prison was built with a deliberate forbidding appearance. In the twentieth century the prison was taken over by Angus County Council and transformed into the offices still known today as County Buildings. The frontage was lightened with larger windows and the forbidding outside wall was demolished. However, some of the bathrooms and store cupboards on the lower floor still retain the heavy prison doors and are referred to as the cells.

Angus was the seat of an ancient kingdom of the Picts and they left behind a wealth of intricately carved stones. Large groups of stones have been found at St Vigeans, Kirriemuir and at Aberlemno. Here the stones remain outside, while many others have been taken into museums for their preservation. Aberlemno has three stones by the roadside, including this stone with carved angels. The parish church is also home to a magnificent stone showing a battle scene on one side and an intricate cross on the other. During the winter the stones are protected from the elements by large boxes.

Improvements and development are nothing new: the late Victorian planners
eagerly cleared away old Georgian and earlier buildings to make way for more
grandiose structures to house banks, halls and other public buildings. This row of
eighteenth-century buildings on Forfar's Castle Street is now the site of the grander
Clydesdale Bank, built around the 1900s.

The Seaforth Hotel was one of the first buildings a visitor to Arbroath would see in the
pre-war era. The hotel is shown here with the new Art Deco indoor swimming pool
still under construction in the 1930s. The house was built in 1817 and was later the
home of the Corsar family of manufacturers. Arbroath Town Council purchased the
Seaforth estate in 1933 to expand their facilities for summer visitors and tourists with
their plan to build an open-air swimming pool. The town council then sold the house
and garden to a consortium of local businessmen, who developed it as a hotel.

The Panmure Arms Hotel in Edzell was the starting point for the popular Glen Bus service. The bus was a large horse-drawn cart holding about a dozen day trippers who enjoyed a leisurely trip to Tarfside in Glenesk and onto Loch Lee. The hotel has been seriously damaged by fire on two occasions, in 1951 and 1958. After the second fire it was restored as a smaller building with only two storeys.

The remains of Scotland's first lunatic asylum now lie under the tarmac of a large chemical plant in Montrose. The asylum was constructed on the northern shore of the River South Esk and opened in 1781. It was a joint institution and was known officially as the Montrose Lunatic Asylum, Infirmary and Dispensary. One of the main movers for such an institution was Susan Carnegie of Charleton, a well-connected patroness of many local good causes. Before this time, lunatics received poor care, with many being housed in the old tolbooth and taken out onto the street to beg for money for their own food. In 1886 the original asylum building was sold to the War Office, who had already been using it as a barracks for some time. A larger asylum was built at Sunnyside, and for a time was the residence of the father of Arthur Conan Doyle, the creator of *Sherlock Holmes*.

The post-Second World War era saw a big push for redevelopment and improvement in towns. In Montrose, one of the areas redeveloped included Castle Street, which had formerly housed a number of grand but dilapidated mansions, including Ramsay House and the adjoining Balmain House. These were the Georgian town houses of local lairds, who frequently chose to spend the long winters enjoying the pleasures of town life, such as the coffee house, the balls in the Guild Hall and the latest productions at the theatre on Bridge Street. Over time the use of these old houses changed and they were often split up into flats. Balmain House once housed a lace school for young girls, and was latterly a bed and breakfast establishment. Both houses were demolished in 1966.

Opposite above: Hedderwick House is an ancient estate situated about two miles north west of Montrose. It was always known for its fine gardens and stately trees. The original seventeenth-century house was built by the powerful Scott family when they acquired the estate around the 1650s. During the 1640s Montrose was governed by Provost James Scott of Logie, nicknamed the Dictator Provost. Scott was a wealthy man, who bought each of his sons an estate in the area including Newmanswalls, Eaglesjohn, Charleton, Craigo, Usan and Hedderwick. Legend tells us that Provost Scott could travel all round the tidal basin of Montrose without ever stepping off Scott land. In the nineteenth century Hedderwick passed though the female line to the Robertsons. They did not live there, instead splitting up the house for use by farm tenants. The house was ruinous by the 1960s and the remainder was flattened in 1984 as a safety precaution.

Opposite below: Montrose is famous for its distinctive closes. The names of the closes change over time, but this one is still known as Review Close and was named after the weekly newspaper whose office was further down the close. The house seen here was once a town house of the Erskine's of Dun. It was not one of the grandest or largest, but it retained much of its original appearance until 1906 when it was restored and improved. The roof lines and window arrangements were altered substantially but the house remains recognisable to this day.

3

PEOPLE

One of the most famous natives of Angus is Lady Elizabeth Bowes Lyon of Glamis, later Queen Elizabeth, consort of King George VI. Much has been made of the Queen's role during the Second World War in supporting morale in the country. Her efforts led Adolf Hitler to refer to her as the most dangerous woman in Europe. She remained one of the most popular royal figures during her lifetime in her roles as both Queen and later as Queen Mother. She died in 2002 aged 101 years.

Princess Elizabeth, the future Queen Elizabeth, visited Angus many times during her childhood with her mother. This sweet image was captured at a local Highland Games by Fred Ferguson, the Town Clerk of Brechin, and a keen amateur photographer.

Harry Lauder, the famous Scottish comedian and entertainer, spent some years during his youth in Arbroath, working in Gordon's Mill and attending its half time school. He made a number of return visits to Angus during the height of his fame, including a 1904 appearance at the Reid Hall, Forfar. In July 1924 he made another flying visit to Arbroath visiting a variety of old friends including John Stewart, manager of the local British Linen Bank and Honorary Secretary of the Cronies Club, and Provost Hanick of Forfar.

Violet Jacob

Scots-language poet and author Violet Jacob was born into the ancient Erskine family of Dun in 1863. She grew up in the Angus countryside absorbing the language and the stories of the area and learnt the Angus dialect from farm servants on the estate. She would later use this in her poetry and in her novels. After her marriage to Arthur Jacob she spent some years in India, where she made a series of watercolour studies of the flora and fauna of the country. These were donated to Edinburgh University, which awarded her an honorary doctorate in 1936. Violet died in 1946.

Hugh MacDiarmid was the pen name of Scots-language poet Christopher Murray Grieve. During the 1920s he was a journalist working for the *Montrose Review* and a member of the town council. During this time he did much to further the movement known as the Scottish Renaissance, which saw a flourishing of writing in the Scots vernacular. In 1926 MacDiarmid published possibly his most famous poem, 'The Drunk Man Looks at the Thistle'. His friend, local sculptor and artist William Lamb, carved his bust in which MacDiarmid's hair is thistle shaped.

Montrose artist George Paul Chalmers was born in 1833, the son of a sailor. After a brief apprenticeship to a ship's chandler, Chalmers left Montrose to follow his true vocation and study art in Edinburgh. Chalmers was a perfectionist in his art and it quickly became known that if you commissioned a painting you should remove it as soon as it pleased you; otherwise Chalmers was known to overdo his painting and spoil it. Chalmers enjoyed a successful career as a portrait painter and later turned to painting landscapes, his real love. This new-found indulgence was to be short-lived. On the evening of 16 February 1878 he was the victim of a violent mugging near Charlotte Square, Edinburgh. Chalmers was taken to the infirmary but he never recovered consciousness and died a few days later.

Montrose artist and sculptor William Lamb began his career as a stonemason, but his passion was for art. As a soldier during the First World War Lamb sustained extensive damage to his right hand. Undeterred by this trauma, Lamb attended Edinburgh College of Art where he taught himself to draw, paint and sculpt with his left hand. After a tour of Europe by bicycle he returned to settle in his native town. In 1932 Lamb was commissioned by Elizabeth, Duchess of York, to model portrait heads of her infant daughters, the Princesses Elizabeth and Margaret Rose. Impressed by his skill, the Duchess also commissioned Lamb to produce a portrait of her. These works are on display together in the William Lamb Studio, which he gave to the town on his death in 1951.

Scientist Robert Watson-Watt was born in Union Street, Brechin, in 1892. He showed an early interest in science, spending many hours experimenting in the workshop of his father's joinery business. Watson-Watt won a scholarship to Brechin High School and later to University College, Dundee, where he took a degree in Electrical Engineering. He became fascinated by the exciting new science of radio. At the beginning of the Second World War he accepted a post in the Government Met Office at Farnborough, where he was asked to find a way to forecast the approach of lightning and thunderstorms to warn aviators. During these studies Watson-Watt realised that aircraft could also be detected. He had discovered the science underlying radar. At first he could detect aircraft up to eight miles away and then up to forty miles. The RAF were very impressed with his work and set up a team of scientists to work on Britain's secret weapon. In 1942, when his work became public, he was awarded a knighthood.

Catherine Hollingsworth was born in Brechin in 1904, daughter of Brechin band leader and well-known musician Henry Hollingsworth. Catherine inherited her father's love of music and entertainment and joined her director father in the Brechin Amateur Operatic Society, taking on roles such as Pittising in the *Mikado*. She is pictured here with David Sherrat in *The Geisha*. Catherine studied at the Royal Academy of Music in London between 1922 and 1925 and later moved to Aberdeen. It was there in 1941 that she founded the first municipal children's theatre in the country, as well as working in the field of speech therapy. She was made a Fellow of the Royal Academy in 1954. She died in July 1999.

John M. Dunn, later Provost of Brechin, was a photographer by trade. He began his working life at thirteen years old on the railway, later moving to Brechin where he held a number of jobs, many simultaneously. One of those jobs was as the Brechin photo correspondent for the *Daily Mail*. Initially he had only a few photographs accepted for publication. In 1908, during a slow news week, he took studies of suffragettes at the Kincardineshire by-election. These studies were the turning point in his photographic career. He became a freelance photographer, commissioned by many of the illustrated press. One commission required him to make a dash to the summit of Ben Nevis by illegally riding a freight train, taking a pony ride and going on foot, so that he could photograph the first ascent of the mountain by a Ford car. Dunn took many local photographs in his career, including political gatherings, railway accidents, shipwrecks, snowstorms, strikes, floods, garden parties and the activities of Brechin Town Council and Queen Mary's visit to Angus in 1921.

Well-known Carnoustie character Granny Fox had numerous children and at the time of her death, on 4 November 1867, she had nearly 200 descendants living locally. Granny Fox was born Cath Adam and was originally from Kirriemuir. She married widowed father of five, Alexander Fox, in Barry in 1801. She was thrifty, industrious, and never idle. Granny Fox acquired a great store of medical knowledge gleaned from having a total of sixteen children to look after. She was happy to share her skill and no birth or burial was complete without her. Granny Fox remained active in her philanthropic activities until six weeks before her death. She is buried in Barry kirkyard.

This study of Jess Cattanach of Whigginton, Glenesk, was captured as she sat by her kitchen fire reading a letter in the early twentieth century. Jess lived and worked on the farm with her bachelor brother (nicknamed Whiggie in the Scottish tradition of calling a man by his land), which her family had farmed for generations. She built dykes, clipped sheep and cut grain, her 6ft-tall frame no doubt being an asset. Jess Cattanach was a much photographed and well-known Glen character. She died on 28 January 1919 in her ninety-seventh year.

A beautiful portrait of young Tibbie Taggart of Brechin in a typical pose adopted by many young children. It was taken by James Waterson, an amateur photographer, in Brechin. Tibbie reputedly grew up to become a schoolteacher.

Peter Reid was known as Forfar's Grand Old Man. Reid inherited his father's grocery business in Castle Street. He started to specialize in a particular kind of confectionery which he made in the back shop. It was to become world famous as 'Peter Reid Rock', or 'Forfar Rock', and it earned him a fortune. Reid spent £25,000 of his fortune on the town of Forfar, an enormous sum at the time. He gifted the town the Reid Hall, benches in the Myre, cast-iron urinals and a convalescent ward at Forfar Infirmary. His final gift was the presentation of a public park for the community, named after him and opened amidst great celebrations. Forfar's Grand Old Man died in 1897 and is buried with his family at Newmonthill Cemetery. He had spent so much of his fortune on others that he died a poor man.

Victorians were fond of photographs of characters as well as celebrities. One such well-known Arbroath character was Alickie Gauldie (1851-1901), seen here on the left of the photograph. Alickie's eccentricities concerning his odd clothing choices were well known in the town. He might wear an overcoat, muffler and carry an umbrella on a wet day and yet be totally unconcerned that his toes were sticking out of his shoes. Despite his rather grubby appearance, Alickie always kept his tenement room scrupulously clean. He was a proud man, refusing all but the most essential of charity. Instead, he preferred to help other people. It is a testament to his character and dignity that he counted the Chief of Police and the Inspector of Poor amongst his friends.

In his younger days James Cobb of Menmuir served as a sergeant in the 93rd Sutherland Highlanders. He fought in the Crimean War, earning medals for his bravery. In 1854 his regiment stormed the height above the Alma River. This was commemorated in Arbroath by the naming of the Alma Works at Francis Webster's weaving mill and sundry other Alma Bars. The 93rd also saw action at Sebastopol and Balaklava. One of the medals on his jacket is the Crimean Campaign Medal, with the others being a Turkish one and a Napoleon 3 Legion of Honour medal. In later life Cobb and his wife Alison lived at the West Links Tollhouse in Arbroath, where his family ran a bicycle hire business for day trippers.

George O'Neill was one of Brechin's Town Officers. Every burgh had at least one and the office of Town Officer was hundreds of years old. By the Victorian era their duties were becoming ceremonial rather than practical. He accompanied the magistrates at the annual water inspections, the riding of the marches and the kirking of the council. Originally Town Officers were burgh employees, who did whatever the magistrates required, from calling councillors to elections to being present at executions.

In 1915 Petty Officer George Samson became the first seaman in fifty years to be awarded the Victoria Cross. Samson had been the first man ashore at the landing at Suvla Bay in the Dardanelles during the First World War. He exhibited great bravery in assisting many of his fellow seamen from the shore to the relative safety of a hopper on 15 April 1915. After exhaustion had led him and two fellow seamen to give up this task, he remained tending the wounded. All this took place under a hail of Turkish bullets and over the course of many hours. The next day Samson suffered multiple wounds while giving covering fire. He had been in action without a break for thirty hours. Samson was born in Arbroath and had subsequently moved to Carnoustie, where a street was named in his honour. He was one of a number of men from Angus to be awarded the Victoria Cross. The other men included Charles Melvin and Lord Lyell, both of Kirriemuir, and Charles Jarvis of Carnoustie. After the war Samson returned to the Merchant Navy.

William Coull Anderson is one example of the Scot who emigrated. William was born and brought up in Arbroath, where his father was a partner in a successful building company, but followed various other members of his family to the American Mid West in the early years of the twentieth century. He became a civil engineer and one of his employers sent him to the Soviet Union in the 1930s, where he helped to build tractors. He enjoyed some breaks at a Black Sea resort and is pictured here with a Black Sea beauty. Anderson was always proud of his Angus origins and made many trips back to visit his relatives in Kydd Street, Arbroath.

Peter Pan's creator J.M. Barrie was born into a Kirriemuir weaving family on 9 May 1860. His mother, Margaret Ogilvy, was a great influence on him, bringing up her family strictly and attending the South Free Church every Sunday. Barrie found inspiration in his mother's tales of her childhood, making up plays with his friends based on her stories. Barrie left Kirriemuir to study in Glasgow, Dumfries and at Edinburgh University. After university he obtained his first writing job on the *Nottingham Journal*, but his services were not required for long and so he returned to his home town. There he drew inspiration from his mother's stories to write articles about the imaginary town of Thrums. His 'Scotch pieces' were a success and he moved to London in 1885 to establish himself as a writer. The rest is history. *Peter Pan* was first performed in 1904 and continues to be performed regularly to this day. Barrie died on 19 June 1937 and is buried at the new cemetery in Kirriemuir.

Barrie's birthplace has drawn many visitors from all over the world to Kirriemuir, including actress Dame Anna Neagle, famous for her film roles as Florence Nightingale, Nell Gwynn, Queen Victoria and Amy Johnston, among others. In 1938 she made a personal appearance in Dundee to promote her new movie *Victoria the Great* and decided to visit Kirriemuir as she had often played Peter Pan on stage. Neagle was accompanied by Herbert Wilcox, the producer and director of many of her films, whom she married in 1943.

4

EVENTS

Arbroath Abbey was the venue for one of the most audacious acts of twentieth-century Scottish history. On the morning of 11 April 1951, Arbroath Abbey custodian James Wishart went to work as usual only to discover that the Stone of Destiny had been placed on the site of the high altar. The Stone of Destiny was the ancient coronation stone of Scotland removed in 1296 by King Edward I of England to Westminster Abbey. On Christmas Day 1950 it had been stolen from Westminster Abbey and a nationwide search launched to trace its whereabouts. After its discovery, the stone was returned to Westminster Abbey until 1996, when it was permanently repatriated to Scotland. The story of the theft was made into a movie, *Stone of Destiny*, directed by Charles Martin Smith, in 2008.

Angus celebrated the coronation of King George VI and Queen Elizabeth on 12 May 1937 with great enthusiasm. Most Angus towns staged competitions for the best decorated street or building. The ladies of West Mill Wynd, Arbroath, pictured here, have obviously worked hard to decorate the buildings with elaborate arrangements of bunting, flags, paper-chains and royal portraits.

A group of Ferryden schoolchildren are enjoying the celebrations attending to the coronation of Queen Elizabeth II on 2 June 1953. The children are sitting in the Fishermen's Hall, enjoying some juice in the cups they had brought with them from home. As part of Ferryden's coronation celebrations the village children were treated to a cinema show in the hall and participated in a sports day at the playing fields, followed by a fancy dress parade to the pier. They also received a souvenir mug.

Montrose Air Station was the first operational military airfield in Britain. It was established by the Royal Flying Corps in 1913 to train pilots for combat duties. A number of original 1913 aircraft hangars still survive and now form a part of the museum. During the First World War the life expectancy of a pilot was just two weeks; some never made it into combat, dying as the result of accidents during training. One such was Desmond Arthur, who died in a flying accident in 1913. His ghost is said to still haunt the aerodrome.

This is a rare image of First World War munitions production at Simpson's Garage in Clerk Street, Brechin in 1917. Until the war the garage had been repairing and making coaches and carriages, acting as selling agents for the Argyle car, repairing cars and selling petrol.

Some men of the Army Service Corps are seen here making bread in the garden behind Montrose Museum. During the First World War a number of ASC service men were stationed at the church halls in nearby Baltic Street. The ASC were a support corps providing land, coastal and lake transport, air dispatch, supplies of food, water, fuel, and general domestic stores such as clothing, furniture and stationery for the military. Their presence in the town may have been linked to the nearby air station. In 1918 the corps added the word Royal to their name.

At the start of the First World War Lady Elizabeth and other members of the Bowes Lyon family returned to Glamis from London to set up a convalescent hospital for wounded soldiers at Glamis Castle, with the Great Hall used as a ward for fourteen soldiers. The men are wearing the light-coloured suits of the convalescent soldier. One man has had his left hand amputated.

The aristocracy of Angus assisted the war effort in their own way. Seated in the centre is Mabel, Dowager Countess of Airlie, a Lady-in-Waiting to Queen Mary. She was a stalwart of the Red Cross in Angus, raising funds for the organisation and promoting its work. Standing behind her is a very young Queen Mother.

The east coast of Angus did not escape German bombing raids during the Second World War. On 20 August 1940 the crew of this German Heinkel 115C floatplane based in Stavanger, Norway crashed on a reconnaissance mission on Fauldiehill, near Arbirlot. Two German crew members died and a third, Lieutenant Tonne, was very seriously injured. He was rescued from the crash and taken to Arbroath Infirmary by a farmer. The most serious raid took place on 25 October 1941, when a number of targets were hit including HMS *Condor* in Arbroath, the air station in Montrose, where six RAF personnel died and twenty injured, and on the town of Montrose. In total it is believed that eighteen bombs were dropped, five of which failed to explode.

A street scene at Brothock Bridge, Arbroath, when Mrs McGregor of Abethune and an unidentified lady companion addressed a suffragette rally in 1918. Most of the crowd appear to be men; only two ladies' hats can be readily identified. The crowd is assembled in front of the site of the present Bank of Scotland with a mill, now the Arbroath Herald building, in the background.

The South Esk River has flooded River Street, Brechin, on numerous occasions, most notably in 1860, 1872, 1913, 1920 and 1949. The floods of May 1913 were unprecedented and were the result of a four-day rainstorm. The area between Bridge Street and the Meikle Mill were inundated and some houses were submerged under 4ft of water. Inhabitants had to be rescued by cart and boat and some had to be temporarily re-housed in the almshouse or the City Hall. The repeated flooding resulted in the old eighteenth- and nineteenth-century buildings being redeveloped in the modern era.

Trinity Road Brechin 2/1/07

A snow storm started on 26 December 1906 and lasted nearly a week, covering the whole of Angus in a deep blanket of snow. Brechin was completely isolated by heavy drifting snow. Telephone and telegraph wires were brought down by the weight of the snow. Businesses were at a virtual standstill as the streets could not be kept clear. Shopkeepers found themselves unable to deliver goods for the New Year festivities.

The deep fall of snow drifted, causing problems on the railways. This railway cutting at Usan near Montrose was completely impassable.

The Elliot Disaster of 28 December 1906 resulted in the deaths of twenty-one people. The local Arbroath-Carmyllie train was stationary at Elliot junction when the Scotch Express crashed into it. The severe snow storm that had started on the 26 December was still continuing and played a part in the accident through poor visibility. The local train was almost completely destroyed by the impact of the express and most of the fatalities occurred on that train.

On 7 August 1912 the American millionaire and philanthropist Andrew Carnegie unveiled a statue in honour of the poet Robert Burns in the Mid Links gardens of Montrose. It had taken many years of fundraising and negotiating to accomplish the goal of erecting the statute to Burns, whose family had Montrose connections. Carnegie had contributed funds on condition that the Montrose statue did not look anything like the one in Central Park, New York, which he disliked.

The Royal Company of Archers visits Montrose every six years. The archers are members of a 300-year-old private archery club based in Edinburgh, who have a ceremonial role as the sovereign's bodyguard in Scotland. This particular visit took place on 30 June 1913, when they competed in the traditional Silver Arrow Competition on the Links. An archer is seen here accompanied by the Provost, three bailies and the Town Officer.

The opening of Forfar's Reid Park on 27 June 1896 was the cause of town-wide celebrations. The park was the gift of Peter Reid, the confectioner. The Reid Park was his final gift to his native town. Shops, businesses and factories all took part in the celebrations to show their gratitude to Reid. The streets were decked in flags, banners, decorated arches and floral displays. The town itself was full of visitors enjoying the grand opening celebrations, with thousands of people travelling by train to Forfar. Reid died the following year, aged ninety-seven.

A crowd has assembled outside the premises of dentist Dr French of East High Street, Forfar, on the day of the opening of the Reid Park in 1896, where one of the many floral displays was set up around the town.

The annual inspection of the water supply was undertaken by most town councils in the early part of the twentieth century as improvements in public health were boosted by the securing of large, clean water supplies for each town.

Brechin's water supply came from the Mooran in Glenesk. Brechin Town Council made an annual water inspection, which involved sampling the water with a picnic lunch. Professional photographer and councillor John M. Dunn recorded many such outings. He took this informal vignette of Provost James W. Addison and Bailie Melrose engaged in a chat with two waitresses.

Burghs have always jealously guarded their boundaries from encroachments by neighbouring landowners and their tenants. They did this by making an annual riding of the marches, or boundaries, to check all fences and boundary markers were in the correct places and to remove any obstacles. Brechin Town Council was amongst the last to continue to perform this yearly ritual. John M. Dunn captured another informal vignette of councillors engaged in studying the burgh boundaries map.

A Scottish burgh can grant the freedom of the burgh to illustrious visitors or inhabitants. On 15 September 1923 HRH the Duke of York, later King George VI, was granted this honour at the Cross of Forfar in front of a large crowd of Forfarians. The officiating magistrate is Provost Moffat. Elizabeth, Duchess of York, looks on from the right of the platform party at her husband. She is sitting beside her father, the Earl of Strathmore. The silver casket on the table was specially made for the occasion to house the Freedom Scroll.

During the Second World War many Crimean War canon, brought back to Britain as war souvenirs, were removed from parks and hills to be melted down for the current war effort. A crowd has gathered to watch such an operation on Arbroath's Boulzie Hill on 19 August 1940.

During the 1950s and '60s a great deal of regeneration work was undertaken in Arbroath and in other towns and cities throughout Scotland. One example of such work is shown here at the Wardmill area of Arbroath, a well-used industrial site. Various workmen are busy pulling down and removing the stone from the demolished mill buildings.

Trinity Market, or Taranty as it is commonly called, was an annual horse fair of long standing. It was held on common land owned by Brechin Town Council on the town's muir. The Town Officers would be used to regulate the event in the days before police constables became common. It was mainly a horse fair, but it attracted showmen's stalls too. Brechin would arrange for its horse-drawn burgh water cart to supply water to the showmen's steam engines at a cost of 1s per cartful.

This traveller lady attending Trinity Market is unaware that she is being photographed. Although this view of the market was taken in around 1912, she could be from any part of the preceding century. She is wearing a plaid shawl and the white bonnet commonly worn by Victorian widows.

Left: Another traveller, or showman, at Trinity Market near Brechin. This gentleman is wearing rough old clothes. His waistcoat has been given the added layer of knitted sleeves.

Below: A panoramic view of Forfar Highland Games in the 1880s, on the Market Muir behind Forfar Prison and the Sheriff Court. Highland Games were largely an invention of the Victorian's romantic view of the Highlands. The view shows the central area with a platform, a blurred figure on the platform, and a row of seats for the judges. There is a small grandstand for a seated audience. A number of stalls selling refreshments and souvenirs are well placed to cater for the crowds. The Games are now known as the Strathmore Games after the venue was moved to Glamis Castle.

A dramatic photograph of the accidental fire which devastated the Reid Hall, Forfar, on 31 January 1941. One fire hose can be seen directing water onto the blaze. Up until this incident the Reid Hall was used to billet Polish soldiers.

In 1904 General William Booth, founder of the Salvation Army, caused quite a stir when he visited Friockheim. His fleet of four motorcars was almost as much of an attraction as he was. General Booth is standing up in the back of a motorcar to address the crowd. The entire village had turned out and various workplaces were closed in his honour. He was invited to Friockheim by Miss Lamb, who had joined the Salvation Army in 1884 aged eighteen years old and who served for sixty-five years in total.

During two weeks in the spring of 1921 the little fishing village of Auchmithie was more like Hollywood when a film crew came to visit. They were filming *Christie Johnston*, a story about a Newhaven fisher girl of the same name. Stewart Rome, the movie's star, had been visiting Arbroath and was invited to take a trip to Auchmithie where he found a perfectly preserved nineteenth-century fishing village, ideal as the location. The villagers and fishermen were recruited as extras. The movie was released in December 1922 and was a modest success. Sadly, no copies appear to have survived.

A view of a troop of Scots Greys on parade outside Arbroath's Town House on the cobbled High Street in the late nineteenth century. They had travelled to Arbroath for a recruitment drive. The cavalrymen have their swords drawn and are at attention. The Greys are wearing their bearskin hats, the only heavy regiment of cavalry to do so.

An Auchmithie fisher wedding was steeped in tradition. Before the couple left the village on the long six-mile walk to the church at St Vigeans, they had already participated in two weeks of rigid customs such as 'the reddin of the house', 'cutting and filling of the ticking' and 'the carrying of the things' to the new house. Traditionally, the fisher wedding procession required a piper, or a fiddler, and a dancer to lead the way for good luck. The whole procession would stop for a wee dram at various places, and maybe have a dance too. The bride is not wearing a white dress, most preferring to buy a new dress they could reuse for Sundays and other special occasions.

Margaret Johnston's wedding to David Spence on 26 September 1895 could not have been more different. She was the eldest daughter of wealthy Montrose fish curer W. Douglas Johnston. While this is not a wedding photograph, it does illustrate some of the lavish decorations put up around the harbour where her father's company, Joseph Johnston & Sons, was based. The harbour side and the company ships were decorated on an extensive scale with flags, streamers and bunting, while the company's trawler, the *Southesk*, was decorated with floral crowns. Ferryden's fishing boats all flew flags in her honour. Many public buildings were also decorated. Employees sent Margaret and her new husband a gift of five silver dishes and in return W. Douglas Johnston treated all 300 employees to a meal and an evening entertainment.

5

WORKING LIVES

Left: There are many photographs of people at work, yet there are only a handful of images of the professional photographers who took these photographs. In the early days of Victorian photography most Angus towns had no more than three professional photographers. Montrose photographer Andrew Kerr, nicknamed Curly Kerr, took this self portrait, posing with his camera, in the late 1860s.

Opposite below: Burnside Quarry was the largest in the Newtyle area. It was opened up in 1883 as a family business to provide stone for road metalling. It was operated by James Mann and his three sons William, David and John, who acted as quarry master. This photograph is from a later era, probably in the 1930s when the quarry was owned by John Gray & Sons, who introduced the steam traction engine to crush and grade the rock.

A group of engineering apprentices from the Arbroath firm of engineers Douglas Fraser & Sons clubbed together for this photograph. While the group had probably cleaned up for the photograph, they still have the aura of a dirty job clinging to them. The boys chose to be photographed in their working clothes, indicating their pride in their job and perhaps commemorating the completion of their apprenticeship. Douglas Fraser had originally started in business in 1832 as a flax and sail canvas manufacturer. By the 1870s the predominance of steam saw the firm encounter many difficulties. This situation was saved when Norman Fraser designed an advanced braiding machine. This in turn led to a greater emphasis on engineering, which turned around the company fortunes. The company was later acquired by Giddings & Lewis and renamed Giddings & Lewis-Fraser Ltd.

In 1885 the new Water Tower in Arbroath was nearly completed. It had been constructed by the unemployed labouring men of Arbroath in an early form of workfare scheme. The tower was designed by Friockheim architect William Gillespie Lamond in the style of a medieval fortress with rusticated red sandstone walls. It is affectionately known as Arbroath's castle, but its real purpose was to provide the town with an adequate, clean water supply. The Water Tower was operational for only twenty years until a larger supply of water became available from Glenogil.

Alexander Shanks & Sons Ltd, Arbroath, was famous for the lawnmowers produced at its Dens Ironworks. The workshop where the machines were produced was nicknamed the Grassie. The Shanks lawnmower was favoured by the rich and titled and their clients included four royal families, sixteen Dukes and fifty-five Earls. By the early 1980s Shanks had diversified into making earth-moving equipment and central-heating systems.

An interior view of Francis Webster's weaving shed in Arbroath from around the end of the First World War. The bunting and garlands may be celebrating the end of the war. The firm was established in 1795, but the weaving activities of the Webster family can be traced to 1758. During the nineteenth century production concentrated mainly on sailcloth. Since the decline in sailing vessels and the rise of the steam ship, the production of tarpaulins for rail and road haulage was developed. The company closed in 1992 and its Alma Works were converted into residential flats.

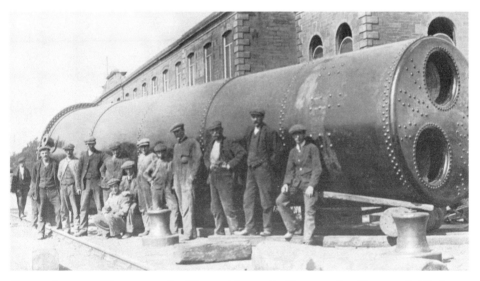

Carnoustie was well known as a healthy seaside resort with a superb golf course, but it also had a reputation for heavy engineering industries. The Panmure Works of James Smieton, established in 1857, is one example. The men are seen here standing beside a newly fabricated boiler for a large steam train. Smieton was an enlightened employer, building many small cottages in the streets surrounding the Panmure Works for his employees. He made them a gift of the Panmure Institute, where he employed teachers. Smieton arranged for the children who worked as half-timers to be instructed in basic skills such as sewing and music.

In 1878 the office staff of James Craik's Manor Works posed for a photograph in the Myre, Forfar, outside the factory. The weaving company was founded by James Craik senior, but it was his sons, James and Alexander, who went on to make the venture a successful one. James junior built the Manor Works factory in 1863 on the reclaimed Myre. The next year he employed 230 hands at 180 power looms. Part of the factory survives to this day as flats.

Before the invention of computers, printing was a labourious job. The staff of the *Brechin Advertiser* are seen here preparing an edition of the weekly newspaper in the 1970s. The first edition had been issued on Monday 10 October 1848 by David Burns. By the 1890s the *Brechin Advertiser* was synonymous with D.H. Edwards, who not only published the newspaper, but also wrote many books on local history.

The smithy at Causewayend, Kinnordy Road, Kirriemuir is just across the road from the entrance to the Lyell of Kinnordy estate. An oversized horseshoe surrounded the front door advertising the service offered. The blacksmith and his family lived in a cottage across the road. The local blacksmith would make everything from traditional horseshoes to pendulums for local clockmakers. The smithy fell into disuse in the early twentieth century, but has since been restored as a home.

Two Brechin wheelwrights in Damacre Road finish off their work on a metal-rimmed wheel by pouring cold water to cool and contract the metal.

A rural garage on the Dundee Road, Newtyle, offering a range of services from repairs to petrol.

Montrose Public Library was opened in 1905 by American millionaire Andrew Carnegie. James Christison, the first librarian, is issuing books from the original issue desk, positioned under the cupola. He held the post for nearly forty years. Montrose had discussed the issue of a public library since 1887. The town already had a Trades Library and a Subscription Library, but these were felt to be insufficient. Between them they had a total stock of 30,000 books, but suffered from a lack of a proper reading room. Many townsfolk were concerned that Montrose was not sufficiently prosperous to afford the increase in rates to support the project, so, in common with many other local authorities in Britain, they approached Andrew Carnegie as a source of funding. He agreed to assist if a suitable site was located and donated £7,500 to build the library. The Free Libraries Act was adopted on 13 January 1902 and the building opened to the public in 1905. It is still in use today.

In the past the post office was often the hub of a community, providing a vital communication service, a shop and some welcome local gossip. The post office at Lintrathen was a good example of a rural office. It was housed in a traditional 'But and Ben cottage' consisting originally of two rooms. The postmaster reputedly enjoyed spending time on his kitchen garden. The post runner, who delivered the mail, a servant, and the postmaster's wife and daughter are also pictured.

This group of 1880s Arbroath postmen have been posed holding letters in their hands. They are wearing the post-1868 style military jacket in dark blue with red piping and the Shako hat with the peak.

Arbroath's Victorian fire engine was a far cry from the fast and powerful machines of today. In 1897 this engine was financed and maintained by the town council, and was one of the last steam-powered fire engines. More efficient combustion engines started to take over around the early 1900s. This particular machine and its crew were captained by manufacturer David Corsar of Cairniehill, seen here in the centre of the photograph. Larger industrial factories often had their own independent fire engine. Low's Foundry in Monifieth had their own fire brigade, and loaned it to the town when needed.

An early twentieth-century Brechin fire crew are shown posing with hoses at the rear of the new fire station on City Road. In the seventeenth century much of the centre of Brechin had been destroyed in a huge conflagration that left wealthy merchant families destitute and without the means to restart their businesses. In the nineteenth century the Brechin fire crew were more organised and better equipped, but the key to the fire engine still had to be obtained from the police office on Church Street before a fire could be tackled. On one occasion they were called to a serious fire at Cortachy Castle during a house party hosted by the Earl of Dudley. The Earl's guests had to be accommodated by the Earl of Dalhousie at Brechin Castle with their servants and horses spread around the hotels, inns and stables of the area. The *Brechin Almanac* noted that such fine horse flesh had never before been seen in the town's stables.

Above: Before the Second World War it was still common to find a police presence in every village. In the early twentieth century Forfar had six constables and two sergeants with Chief Constable James Stirling in charge. They didn't often have to deal with serious or violent crime. Sergeant Doig, sitting to the right of the chief constable, arrested James Laing in October 1903 on suspicion of causing the death of chimney sweep James Carrie after a drunken assault. Carrie died from head injuries after five days. A week after his arrest Laing was released from jail as there was insufficient evidence of murder to proceed.

Right: G.H. Strachan, sheriff officer in Arbroath, astride his tricycle, 1889. Strachan was not only a sheriff officer, but also a constable and a Town Officer. He worked from his office at 1 Hill Terrace, still in use today as council offices. The 1890s saw a huge explosion of interest in pedal power, and the rise in popularity of all things cycling.

Road mending is a never-ending task. This road crew are mending the roads in Monifieth.

A young Edwardian girl is standing on the back of the horse-drawn cart used to deliver the milk from Mrs Fitchett's Rosehill Dairy, Montrose. Householders would come out to the cart with a jug to be filled. The dairy was one of two operating from the Rosehill area in the late nineteenth/early twentieth century. Rosehill was then on the edge of the town's built up area. Alexander Fitchett started the business, but after his death in 1902 the dairy was continued by his widow. This photograph was taken on Northesk Road, with the large houses of the Mall behind the railings.

William Culbert, originally from Aberdeen, was one of Arbroath's many street sellers. He was nicknamed Stumpie by the local folks because he had a false leg. Despite this handicap, he managed his barrow of fruit and vegetables around the streets. He enticed people to buy his oranges with a cry of 'Sweet Seville oranges, nane o' yer foreign dirt here.'

David Arthur, another Arbroath street trader, was more fortunate. He carried on his knife- and scissor-grinding business with the help of a donkey-drawn cart.

The River North Esk, to the north of Montrose, is a good salmon fishing river. Joseph Johnston & Sons Ltd held the salmon fishing rights for over 100 years, establishing many fishing stations along the river and its estuary. This particular catch took place in front of a good crowd of spectators under the old railway bridge across the North Esk.

Water mills provided an early source of power for machinery and industrial developments often began along streams and rivers. Some streams supported a large number of mills before the advent of steam-power. This is the former meal mill at Arbirlot, once part of a thriving village community comprising a slaughterhouse, a church, two schools, a post office, a savings bank, an inn and a parish library, in addition to a number of shops.

The *Lochside II* was a popular boat in Montrose, not least because it was known as 'The Beerie'.
Here it is moored at the quayside in Montrose harbour waiting to transport the beer barrels
produced by the Lochside Distillery at the top of Northesk Road. The steam-powered coaster
could carry about 1,500 barrels of beer on its regular route between the port of Montrose and
the Tyne. The *Lochside II* operated the route for thirty years until she was sold onto another
owner in 1955. Lochside Distillery was demolished some years ago, replaced by housing.

The 1930s was the golden age of the cinema. The staff of the new Picture House on the High
Street, Arbroath, are shown here ready to open the doors of the new cinema on Christmas
Day 1930. The first programme included the all-singing, all-dancing movie *Chasing Rainbows*,
which included the hit song 'Happy days are here again'. Most importantly for such a grand
opening, the movie was an early colour movie. The usherettes are wearing fashionable
uniforms, while one of the ushers is wearing his military medals for the photograph.

A lady shopkeeper, perhaps Mrs Johnston, is standing in the entrance to Johnston's Grand Emporium on the corner of the High Street and James Street, Arbroath, in the late 1920s. The Emporium was one of those old-fashioned shops where you could buy a wondrous range of goods. Above the door is the slogan 'The house for everything' and the window displays seem to agree. The windows are full of china mugs, wicker baskets, and little wooden wheelbarrows for children. The passer-by is invited to join the Christmas Club.

Bailie William Donaldson of Monifieth owned a shoe shop on the south side of Tay Street. It was more familiarly known as Bailie Tackets' shop. He is pictured in the centre of the photograph along with Tom Whyte of the Fountainbrae Nursery, and John Nicoll of the burgh's Cleansing staff.

It is rare to find interior views of bars from the Victorian era, and even rarer to see a lady publican. Mrs Agnes Oram is shown standing behind the gleaming bar of the Crown Inn on West Abbey Street, Arbroath. After the death of her husband in 1899, she took over the running of the inn and continued as a publican until her death in 1924. An inn was a larger public house offering food, stabling, and a variety of dining and meeting rooms to hire. Hours were long, with the staff working at least ten hours per day and often up to 100 hours per week. Pay was low, but food and accommodation were provided.

Before the Second World War, it was common to find porters from hotels waiting at the railway stations to collect passengers, in order to convey luggage and guests on to their hotel. Arbroath hotel porters from the Royal Hotel, the White Hart Hotel, and another hotel are seen here waiting for business. Each man is dressed in a suit and wearing a hat emblazoned with the name of his establishment. The White Hart Hotel porter was William Gardiner. The White Hart was originally the principal coaching inn of the town. At one time it was run by two sisters, the Misses Fildan, who hosted evening parties for the officers of the press gangs which operated in the area during the Napoleonic era.

FINISHED FOR THE DAY.

Handloom weaving had been the cottage industry which gave Angus a boost into the industrial era. Every village and hamlet had its share of weavers, with the looms housed in attics. In time these individuals began to come together in factories such as those of Francis Webster in Arbroath, the Wilkie's in Kirriemuir, the Duke's in Brechin, Paton's in Montrose and the Craik's in Forfar. As the factory system took over and looms were powered by steam, the solitary handloom weaver began to disappear by the beginning of the twentieth century.

Opposite above: Many of the Ferryden girls, who worked at Paton's Mill in Montrose, would take the ferry over the River South Esk to and from work. Many would also use this route to go home for lunch. This was the shortest route as the trip over the bridges would lengthen their working day considerably. The ferry was a large rowing boat, open to the elements, and the girls are tightly wound up in their shawls against the weather. They appear to be landing at the Montrose side of the river.

Opposite below: The Monifieth to Dundee tramway was opened on 27 December 1905 by the Dundee, Broughty Ferry & District Tramways Co. The new line extended the city of Dundee tram system from Claypots Road, Broughty Ferry, to the west end of Monifieth's High Street. The trams were decorated with bunting on their first run to the original terminus at the foot of Union Street, near to Troup the Chemist. The tramline was extended six months later to the end of the High Street, terminating outside the Royal Hotel. The total cost of the tramway was £100,000. The trams operated for twenty-six years until the service closed on 15 May 1931.

6

FISHING

Mrs West from Ferryden is seen here collecting mussels along the River South Esk in 1912. The fishwives and their children had to ensure a plentiful supply of mussels for baiting the fishing lines. Montrose Basin was a great source of mussels. Villages such as Auchmithie were further removed from the source of mussels and either had to buy them in or collect more locally available limpets. Mrs West's son Joe wrote one of the few histories of local fishing called *A Personal History of Ferryden*.

David Swankie is reddin the lines, or cleaning them, prior to baiting them with mussels. Swankie is one of the old Arbroath fisher names along with Spink, Cargill, Smith and Beattie. Swankie is working from the skull, or oval wicker basket, on his left with the clean line and then placing the baited line in a skull on his right. This was normally the work of the women and children of the family and of any fisherman who no longer went to sea.

Every boat had two fishing lines; one in use fishing and the other at home being baited. Every line had 1,400 hooks, each needing two mussels to be placed on it, which had to be collected and shelled in advance. Shelling was a monotonous task and best done in the company of others. Baiting the lines took priority over housework in fisher households. It was traditional for fishermen to marry within their own community as they needed a wife who had been brought up to the hard work of fishing. These women are from River Street, Ferryden. The sheds are upturned decommissioned fishing boats.

Auchmithie Smokies are now protected under the European Union's Protected Food Name Scheme. The smokie is a lightly smoked haddock. The process of making smokies was captured by Victorian amateur photographer John Fraser. An Auchmithie fishwife, wearing her oldest clothes, is preparing the fire to smoke the fish. The smoking barrels are sunk into the ground with old whisky barrels preferred. On the ground is kindling wood and a bottle of what appears to be whisky.

The haddock have been decapitated, gutted, sun dried for a few hours and then tied together in pairs. They are then placed over the smoke sticks within the barrel and its a hardwood fire.

The fish are now ready to be covered and smoked.

Once all the fish are on the smoke sticks, the fire is covered with sawdust and the barrels are covered and sealed with wet jute sacks. The fish are smoked for about forty minutes. This process creates a very hot heat and dense smoke which, combined, gives the smokie its unique taste.

A girl and her mother are watching and learning the smoking process. Racks of smoked fish are drying in the open air behind them.

Once the fish had been made into smokies, the work of the fishwife was still not finished: she now had to put on her basket and sell the smokies. Many of them walked long distances to sell their fish. The more modern fishwife might use the railway to reach more distant markets. They wore the distinctive fisher clothing of striped aprons, short pintucked skirts, often with floral blouses. This unknown fishwife is striking an unusual pose by offering her fish to the photographer.

Boats from Montrose and Arbroath followed the herring, making the trip down to Great Yarmouth every summer. A group of women would follow the boat to pack the herring in barrels. One Montrose photographer, John Brown, joined a herring boat on its journey south and made a series of postcards of the herring fishing. This view is called 'Toilers of the Deep' and shows the Ferryden boat the *Anne Mearns*. On the reverse, someone has noted that the young boy, Nicoll, was later killed at Ypres during the First World War.

Herring fishing became popular in the middle of the nineteen century, driven by large fish-curing companies such as Joseph Johnston & Sons of Montrose. Herring could not be smoked, instead it had to be salt pickled in barrels. This is one such herring packing crew in operation at Arbroath harbour, mainly comprising young girls in this instance. They are wearing long leather aprons to protect them from the brine and have their sleeves rolled up for the same reason. The process of packing involved the women working in a team of three, two gutting the herring with a sharp knife while the other one packed the barrel.

When the men followed the herring shoals down the east coast of England they took the opportunity to buy gifts for their wives and sweethearts. China was especially popular, as can be seen from the fine display on the mantelpiece of the kitchen in the Marketgate home of Mr and Mrs Shepherd in the 1920s. Young girls following the fleet as part of a packing crew would also buy china for their dowry and the carrying of the bride's dishes and china from her parent's house to her new home was one of the cornerstones of a traditional fisher wedding.

Lifeboat crews were frequently drawn from the fishing community. Mr Swan is shown here wearing two medals over his fisherman's guernsey with its unique pattern. His son, however, is dressed for the office, perhaps showing a move away from the family's traditional occupation. His wife, seated with a little child, is wearing a more fashionable dress than you might expect, with a fancy black lace collar, teamed with the traditional stripped fisher apron. In contrast her mother-in-law is dressed entirely within the fisher tradition, with the addition of a white bonnet. Swan is one of the less common Auchmithie fisher names and derives from the Anglo-Danish 'Sweyn'.

7

COUNTRYSIDE

The countryside can be seen either as a rural idyll, or a place where the work was hard and the returns could be poor. Idyllic views were promoted by photographers eager to sell prints and postcards. The husband and wife professional photography partnership of William and Isabella Anckorn of Arbroath was internationally renowned for genre scenes such as this. They employed a painterly style that was unlike their local contemporaries. This is a beautifully composed scene signed by Mrs Anckorn, featuring children at Kelly Den, near Arbirlot, around 1890.

The Scots are renowned for their love of porridge, and oats have always formed an important part of the diet. This young man is obviously enjoying a walk in the countryside in autumn and is posing in an oat stook. The oats were cut and dried in the field before they were threshed and sent for milling. A farmer would give his workers a term's supply of both potatoes and oatmeal. The meal was kept in a special kist, or chest. Traditional Scottish oat cakes were easy to take into the fields. Oatmeal broth was also made by cooking the oatmeal in a pot with onions and any spare bits of potato boiled together to make a thick broth. The most famous oatmeal dish is porridge, made by adding water and cooking the mixture, finishing off with a sprinkle of salt.

These ploughmen, believed to be from the Carmyllie area, are pausing for a photograph along with a visitor in a suit. They are working the binder, which cuts and binds the oat into sheaves which are then placed upright into stooks to dry and ripen off. The farmer obtained his farm labourers at the half-yearly feeing markets in May and November. Hired men lived in the farmer's bothy, which comprised of fairly basic accommodation, and a supply of certain foodstuffs. Married servants were hired for a year, and their wives and children put to work at harvest time for a very small wage.

This busy group of farm workers are bringing in the grass harvest at an unidentified farm in the Arbroath area. A heavy horse is pulling cut grass on a sled, known as a tumbling tam, while some of the men are engaged in building the hay cole to provide animals with winter feed. Another man is sitting on top of the horse-drawn hay rake, probably posed for the photograph, as the two processes were not usually performed simultaneously. A young boy wearing dungarees and a young girl wearing an overcoat, possibly the farmer's children, also seem to be present for the benefit of the photographer.

This rural scene is on the outskirts of St Vigeans, where a ploughman is at work with a two-horse team on the east side of the main railway line. The first mass-produced tractor was launched in 1917 by Henry Ford, his Fordson model being manufactured in England. In the background is the pretty village of St Vigeans with its ancient church on top of the hill, where many carved Pictish stones have been found.

An early form of farm mechanisation was the threshing mill which separated the grain from the chaff. It was driven by a traction engine and manned by a regular crew of mill men who took it to all the farms in the area and who expected to be fed at every farm they visited. Threshing day was the hardest day's work on the farm, taking approximately twelve people to successfully complete the operation. It was considered to be man's work, but there are two women in this picture, on top of the threshing mill, loosening the twine on the sheaves to be threshed, which they handed to the man feeding the mill. Other men were engaged in stoking the boiler, carrying bags of grain to be stored, or building the stacks from the straw.

This image shows a group of Glenesk children trying to make hay stacks from the freshly cut grass. It looks to be very heavy work.

Potato planting on such a large scale was not a regular practice in Montrose, but during the First and Second World Wars all available garden space was utilised to grow crops. On 30 April 1917 Montrose's special constables were drafted in to plant potatoes in a field near to the now demolished Newfield House. This area is unrecognisable today, as it is now covered by the swimming pool, built in the 1950s, and a post-war housing estate.

Agricultural shows form a vital part of the local Angus economy, and many, such as the prestigious Angus Show, have been established for more than a century. This horse at a Kirriemuir Agricultural Show deservedly won first prize.

The farms in the Forfar area bought or sold their cattle in the octagonal sales room of the former Auction Mart near to the railway station. It was established on this site in 1879 when it was built as Scott & Graham's Mart. In previous centuries the cattle market and the slaughterhouse were both located in the centre of Forfar, a situation that was not very healthy for the inhabitants. The understanding of public health issues improved during the nineteenth century, necessitating the relocation of such facilities. The Mart adjoined the railway for convenience in shipping goods into and out of the town. The empty carts on Carseview Road are awaiting business from the next train.

While the men were employed in ploughing and field activities, the women on the farm were engaged in other, no less important jobs. One of their main tasks was to keep the men well fed. In addition, they undertook other traditional jobs such as making butter, collecting eggs, milking cows and working in the fields at harvest time. Three generations of women are pictured here busy feeding the farm chickens.

Right: Soft fruit was once a vital part of the Angus agricultural economy, and has enjoyed a resurgence in the early twenty-first century with the advent of poly tunnels and Eastern European migrant workers. For generations, local children had gone to the berries in their summer holidays to make some extra money. They picked raspberries and strawberries all day for a few shillings. Most of the fruit was destined for jam making or for canning. This scene was captured 100 years ago. The lady seems absorbed in her fruit picking and unaware of the photographer. She is wearing arm protectors to prevent the raspberries from staining her sleeves.

Below: Two young girls are captured while working in the raspberry fields. Travelling families were also a large part of the berry-picking workforce. Picking soft fruit has traditionally been a way for younger people to earn some much needed money over the summer.

Seasonal work such as berry picking attracted many travellers to the area in the summer months. Many travelled by foot, or in a horse-drawn caravan, to encampments used by their families for many generations. This family is living in the shelter of a bow-camp tent, a traditional traveller home made from bowed hazel sticks bent and stuck into the ground over which canvas or tarpaulin is stretched. The boys appear to be wary of the photographer.

Another view of a traveller encampment showing both tents and horse-drawn caravans. As the travellers passed through an area they provided a cheap flexible workforce. In addition, they also had products to sell. They made lanterns and milkhouse utensils as well as baskets and horn spoons.

A rare informal study of a piper playing the lamentation for the dead, or coronach in the Highland tradition, at a fellow traveller's funeral. This was captured by John M. Dunn, probably in the Brechin area in the early years of the twentieth century.

Glenesk was a popular destination for day trippers as well as the hunting, fishing and shooting crowd. The Glen Bus from Edzell made it easy for trippers to enjoy a horse-drawn carriage ride through beautiful scenery and perhaps finish their day with a boat trip on Loch Lee at the head of the glen. In this particular 1880s view the boat trip appears to have been more attractive to the men than the women, who have largely remained on shore.

The concept of the day trip is about 130 years old, and started with the introduction of bank holidays in 1871, coupled with a cheap and extensive rail network. This allowed people to enjoy a day out at the seaside or in the countryside. Edzell was well placed to cater to people who wanted to travel up beautiful Glenesk to Invermark and Loch Lee beyond. The Glen Bus set off from the old Panmure Arms Hotel in Edzell. The bus is a horse-drawn open carriage pulled by four horses with rows of open seats. At least one of the passengers was the Glen postman, as indicated by his Shako cap.

Cottar farmers, such as David Stewart, lived in Glenesk in stone-built cottages that were already old when they were photographed. Winters could be harsh in the glens, but David Stewart does not appear to have any special clothes to keep out the extreme cold; the clothes he is wearing are old, ill-fitting and torn.

This cottage is of the traditional But and Ben style, with people living in one half and the animals living in the other during the winter. Some glen houses were a little larger, with a room and a kitchen plus the cow byre. David Stewart's cottage has a timeless interior with the old fashioned hangin' lum style of open chimney.

At the end of a hard day at work, this is the type of cottage that David Stewart would return to. It lacks modern comforts and shows an interior straight out of the eighteenth century.

The Sanatorium, Auchterhouse.

The countryside was also considered to be a healthy place for rest and recuperation after illness. A sanatorium was built near Auchterhouse in 1902 on land donated by the Earl of Airlie. Before the discovery of antibiotics, plenty of rest with fresh air and sunshine were considered beneficial in the treatment of tuberculosis and so balconies and terracing were a feature of sanatoriums, allowing patients easy access to the sunshine. The sanatorium at Auchterhouse catered for all of Angus and the nearby city of Dundee. It later became an ordinary hospital before closing its doors in 1980.

Opposite above: In the Angus glens peat cutting provided the major source of fuel for domestic heating and cooking. Wood was in short supply, and it was expensive to bring in coal. Traditionally, peat cutting was a communal activity, taking place in May and June. Each family would make a peat stack to last them through the winter. This man is cutting peat on the moor with a special spade called a flaughter spade, which was long and flat. The peat would then be carried away on a horse-drawn sled to be stacked, dried and then either used as fuel or as a fertilizer.

Opposite below: Hunting and shooting was very important to the economy of the glens and estate owners built hunting lodges to accommodate hunters and host large parties. Organised grouse shootings became common in the area around the 1880s, and deer stalking became more important as an income, as the price of wool declined. Scotland's most famous and successful deerstalker was Montrose-born Horatio Ross of Rossie, who combined his love of sport with his other love, that of photography, by taking hundreds of photographs of deer in the hills, both before and after he shot them.

8

RECREATION

A group of Montrose bowlers, complete with formal stove-pipe hats and bow ties, are playing
on the old bowling green in 1864. The green was located behind Montrose Museum. A
bowling green had existed on this site since the 1760s. Before the advent of lawnmowers
(invented by Arbroath man Alexander Shanks), the grass on bowling greens was quite rough,
unlike the immaculate greens of today.

Lawn tennis was created in the late 1860s, with rules based loosely on the earlier royal game of real tennis. This tennis party at Balnaboth, Glen Prosen, was taken in the early 1880s. Two ladies are ready to play a game of tennis, while the older women appear to be spectators. During this period no special clothes were worn for the sport but ladies managed a gentle game, despite the tight corsets and high-heeled shoes.

The grass on this tennis court may not reach the standards of the Centre Court at Wimbledon, but it was the pride and joy of Newtyle at the beginning of the twentieth century. The first tennis court was located at the north end of the junction of Commercial Street and Bulb Farm Road, later relocating to the public park. The men are using the old style wooden racket with the flattened head.

Newtyle's quoiting enthusiasts used a piece of spare ground on the south of Church Street as their pitch. Quoits are more commonly associated with England but it enjoyed popularity in some parts of Scotland from the 1880s to the 1930s. The game is similar to fairground hoopla: the player throws a metal ring over a set distance to land on a pin. Many towns had a quoiting club. Brechin's club met in the public park twice a week, and competed for a monthly medal.

A large group of mid-1860s' golfers in Montrose are shown posing at an unidentified tee. In 1818 the first tee was located just beyond St Peter's Episcopal Church. The original course followed a different route, mainly in the southern part of the Links and ran close to the town's grammar school, which was on the site now occupied by Montrose Museum. The course route was altered after the Caledonia railway line bisected the course in 1846. The two boys carrying a large number of wooden golf clubs are the course caddies.

Carnoustie is one of the jewels of Scotland's sporting heritage and one of the best courses in the world. A group of players are on the course near Barry Burn, prior to its modernisation in 1926 by James Braid, a five-time Open champion and esteemed golf course designer. The buildings behind the course, from extreme right to left, include the Bruce Hotel, the Dalhousie Golf Club, now demolished, and Simpson the golf club maker.

Carnoustie's Giant Slide was built in 1929 and was popular with both children and adults. Rumour has it that adults had to be banned from the slide to let the children have a turn! This particular postcard was sent by a young girl named Rosemary, who described the rock pools and shells with pleasure, but who did not care for the seagulls which were 'not tame'.

The paddling pool at Carnoustie was a favourite place for summertime fun and games in the water. Carnoustie Town Council employed an entertainment officer, who organised pool games, car treasure hunts, beauty and talent contests, as well as sporting competitions for the summer visitors. Bill Cumming filled this office for many years and provided happy memories for many holidaymakers. The paddling pool was the venue for 'scrambles'; this was particularly popular with children who, if they were quick enough, could scramble for a share of the half pennies thrown into the pool. The pool and its adjacent shelter were built in the early 1930s. It was closed in the 1970s due to concerns about the quality of the water supply from the Lochty Burn.

In 1925 the summer entertainers at Carnoustie were The Rebels, led by local man Alex Webster. He was working as the manager of the Pavilion, the local cinema in Park Avenue, Carnoustie. Webster was an experienced national performer, being one half of an act called Alberta Flahey & Partner. He travelled to London to secure the best acts for the summer season. The Rebels performed in a comfortable pavilion, and wore gorgeous costumes, with no expense spared, including this updated version of the old Edwardian Pierrot-style costumes from which seaside entertainers drew their nickname.

Earlier Pierrots had operated from a makeshift hut using straw bales to mark out the area for the paying audience. It may seem rough and ready, but a season with the Carnoustie Pierrots was a desirable engagement as it was seen as a stepping stone to greater things. Gilbert Payne's White Coons held the pitch for many years before it was taken over by Leo Bliss and his Busy Bees. Bliss used the slogan 'After fourteen years of Payne, you need a little Bliss' to entice his audience. Bliss was a well-known comedian and star of pantomime in his day.

Beach fashions have changed considerably since the Edwardian era, when adult bathers were required to be covered from the neck to the ankles, with arms covered too. In 1907 an Australian underwater ballerina caused a sensation in the USA by performing in a swimsuit which exposed her neck, arms and legs. Her subsequent movie appearances led to the growing popularity, and acceptance of, skimpier swimming suits by the 1920s. This photograph probably dates from the late 1910s as the lady's suit already exposes her arms and finishes at her knees.

The beach at Montrose was a busy place in the summer. The town was one of many popular east-coast holiday towns promoting a healthy holiday in the fresh air, a welcome contrast to the dirty, smoky air in many towns and cities. The beach was the focus of holiday activities. Sea bathing in the fresh waters of the North Sea was considered to be very beneficial to your health. Bathing machines were installed by the town council to allow visitors to change into their bathing costumes while being gently towed into the water. The income from bathing machines provided a useful boost to the town's funds.

The seafront at the West Links, Arbroath, has always been a busy place, and much enjoyed by families sitting in the sun enjoying picnics, while watching the children paddling and playing at the water's edge. The shelter in the centre was commonly referred to as the White Elephant. The later construction of sea defences has changed the appearance of this part of the beach.

The simple pleasures of a bucket and spade on a sandy beach are all that most children need. Beach wear for children has certainly changed over the years. Despite their interesting range of clothing styles, these children are enjoying a typical day out at the seaside.

Kerr's Miniature Railway has delighted holidaymakers since it was opened in 1935. It has been run continuously by the Kerr family since its creation. One of the first trains was the Flying Scotsman miniature steam engine. This photograph was probably taken during its first year of operation in 1935 as the original 7.5in gauge track is still in use; this was replaced by a wider gauge in 1936. The railway has carried over 1.5 million passengers since it opened.

Motorbike racing on the sands of Monifieth was very popular in the 1930s. Those involved included Provost Tyndall, with the arm band, and next to him 'Bummy' Crichton, the joint owner of a garage in Brook Street. In the late eighteenth and early nineteenth centuries horse racing had been very popular in both Montrose and Monifieth. The Honourable William Maule of Panmure was the patron of the Monifieth Races and provided trophies for the winner. The races took place in the spring and summer. The day ended with a dinner and a ball in Dundee. The races fell into decline and ceased by 1830. In 1839 they were briefly revived in front of 30,000 spectators, many of whom arrived by the new railway, but stopped again by 1841.

Some people preferred to race cars rather than horses and to test them off road. This is a sizeable gathering in one of the Angus glens for a hill race.

Above: During the 1930s Arbroath Town Council made a determined effort to provide increased attractions for visitors. When the council had the opportunity to purchase the Seaforth estate, whose land ran alongside the coast, they jumped at it and put in motion a plan to build a large open-air bathing pool. It opened in 1934 and was popular from the outset.

Right: The open-air swimming pool in Arbroath ran a series of illuminated bathing spectaculars. Here a fireworks display is in progress, framing the diver on the highest diving board. After the Second World War Scottish seaside towns never quite recaptured the glory of the inter-war years. Over time the grandeur of the pool, and its attendance figures, diminished. The pool was sold in 1981.

Brass band concerts were popular events and most towns had a purpose-built bandstand in a public park, or another prominent area. Carnoustie built their bandstand on the Links. The Carnoustie Brass Band of 1895 wore military-style band uniforms. The bandstand programme regularly featured Sunday afternoon concerts by the Burgh Band, playing both religious and military music. In 1924 an evening concert was introduced, which featured a programme of dance music.

When the circus came to town, the town would soon know about it. The performers would arrive in style with a parade through the town, traditionally led by the elephants. This unidentified circus is travelling down Nursery Road, Montrose, and turning into Rosehill Road as they travel to their pitch on the Links. Legend has it that circus elephants coming into Montrose from the south were too heavy to be allowed to walk over the suspension bridge, instead having to travel around the Basin. The elephants may have preferred a visit to Brechin, where they were able to wash and play in the River South Esk, a startling sight for passers-by.

Above: Amateur dramatics were taken very seriously in the Edwardian era, and this was reflected in the quality of the costumes. The cast of a Brechin Sunday School production of *Snow White* are wearing elaborate costumes, decorated with sashes of flowers. The boys are mainly dressed as dwarves, with false beards and hoods. One girl stands in the middle wearing a veil while the little boy in front of her has rebelled and taken off his beard and hood.

Right: Fishing on the river is a timeless activity. These boys are fishing in the River South Esk at Brechin; they are standing on the embankment created in the 1880s to help prevent the river flooding River Street. The medieval bridge can be seen in the distance. Until its construction, the only route over the South Esk to either Montrose or Arbroath was by way of the Ford Mouth at the Inch.

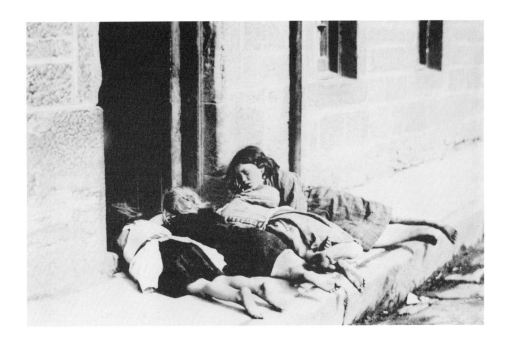

Above: On a hot summer day there is nothing better than to enjoy the sunshine. These barefoot Victorian girls are doing just that at a doorway in River Street, Brechin.

Left: In the 1890s cycling became a very popular sport. This young man is holding a safety bike with pneumatic tyres, which allowed a more comfortable ride. It may be a Kalac cycle, manufactured locally in Forfar by Messrs Patullo & Killacky at a cost of £11 10s. Forfar supported three bicycling clubs before the First World War. The Angus Cycling Club, under the patronage of Thomas Munro of Lindertis, had forty-five members in 1898.

Brechin Photographic Society has been an active society for more than 100 years. In the early years of the twentieth century they organised regular photographic camping trips to Glenesk. Provost John Dunn of Brechin, a member of the society, had purchased a cottage at Haughend, allowing society members to camp there at weekends. Dunn is shown here eating his dinner. The photographers obtained milk from a local farmer, and brought all their other supplies, such as the beer and the teapot. To keep their food from predators, it was strung up on a nearby tree branch.

The landowners in the various Angus glens discovered that they could earn an excellent income by letting the rights to hunt and fish on their land. Many hunting lodges were built in the Victorian era to accommodate parties of hunters, including this unusually shaped lodge at Knockshannoch, Glenisla. The lodges employed many local men as gamekeepers or as grouse beaters. The hunting lodges also generated jobs for the Glens' women as cooks and housemaids.

Some winters can be very severe and one enterprising Kirriemuir lady solved the issue of slippery streets by using her skis to navigate the High Street. One of the most severe winters was that of 1906.

Opposite above: Curling was invented in medieval Scotland and has remained a favourite winter sport to this day. A game that began with the monks of Paisley soon became a particular favourite game of Scottish farmers in their quieter season. Two teams of four people traditionally played on a frozen pond or loch. Their meetings were known as bonspiels.

Opposite below: The Angus Bonspiel took place in January of 1910 on the frozen waters of Forfar Loch. It was the first time the tournament had taken place in eight years. Thirty rinks were set up to accommodate 240 competitors. The gentleman in the centre with the beard and moustache is Provost William Ferguson of Brechin. The earliest Angus curling club formed in Forfar around 1797 and used the loch for its games. Kirriemuir was not far behind, forming a club in the very early years of the nineteenth century. From the middle of the twentieth century purpose-made curling ponds became more common and were much safer.

Other titles published by The History Press

The Guide to Mysterious Glasgow
GEOFF HOLDER

This is the essential guide to everything strange, marvellous, mysterious and paranorm
Glasgow. As well a complete guide to all of the city's gargoyles, legends and relics, it inc
tours of the Necropolis, the cathedral, museums, and all of Glasgow's hidden archaeolc
wonders. Illustrated by more than 100 photographs and filled with countless strange
from the links between St Mungo, Merlin and werewolves to the urban legends c
Glasgow Underground, it will transform the way you experience the city.

978 0 7524 4826 8

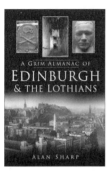

A Grim Almanac of Edinburgh & The Lothians
ALAN SHARP

Beneath the surface respectability of Edinburgh's grand streets lies a warren of filth-r
alleys and stairs where thieves, murderers and ghouls of every description planned and c
out their foul deeds. In this book we meet them all. Major Weir, the devil-worshi
black magician and his wicked sister Grizel; Deacon Brodie, the inspiration behind *Dr
and Mr Hyde*; and of course, worst of all, Mr Burke and Mr Hare, who plied their swift
in corpses for the dissection table of Dr Knox.

978 0 7509 5105 0

Edinburgh Memories
MILES TUBB & JOHN MCCAUGHIE

Edinburgh Memories is the unique and fascinating result of many conversation
interviews with local people, recalling life in their city between the two world wars
memories are recounted, including childhood and schooldays, work and play, spo
leisure. Everyone who knows Edinburgh, as a resident or a visitor, will be amuse
entertained, surprised and moved by these stories, which capture the unique sp
Scotland's capital city.

978 0 7905 5100 5

The Highland Railway
KEITH FENWICK AND HOWARD GEDDES

Illustrated with 200 superb photographs, this book depicts the rich scenery and l
of the Highland Railway, which stretched from Pert via Inverness to Wick and Th
distance of over 260 miles. Despite several attempts to close them, these lines remair
today, but the various branches and the old main line north of Aviemore have disapp
This volume will be a treat for everyone who remembers the golden age of trainsp
and for anyone keen to capture the essence of those bygone days.

978 0 7509 5094 7

Visit our website and discover thousands of other History Press books.
www.thehistorypress.co.uk